MULTILATERALISM OR REGIONALISM?

TRADE POLICY OPTIONS
FOR THE EUROPEAN UNION

GUIDO GLANIA
JÜRGEN MATTHES

CENTRE FOR EUROPEAN POLICY STUDIES
BRUSSELS

The Centre for European Policy Studies (CEPS) is an independent policy research institute based in Brussels. Its mission is to produce sound analytical research leading to constructive solutions to the challenges facing Europe today. The views expressed in this report are those of the authors writing in a personal capacity and do not necessarily reflect those of CEPS or any other institution with which the authors are associated. They gratefully acknowledge financial support provided by DaimlerChrysler and BASF.

Guido Glania, Dr. rer. pol., is responsible for trade and development policy at the Federation of German Industry (BDI), with which he has worked in Brussels since 2004 and in Berlin from 1999-2003. From 1996-99 he was responsible for European trade policy at the Central Federation of the Textile Industry (Gesamttextil) in Eschborn. He studied economics in Cologne and was conferred a doctorate in Erlangen-Nuremberg.

Jürgen Matthes is a Senior Economist with the Cologne Institute for Economic Research (IW Köln). Since 2003 he has been responsible for the International Economic Policy department. Prior to that he was the head of IW's New Economy department (from 2000-03) and personal assistant to the director (1995-2000). His economic studies were undertaken in Dortmund and Dublin. He has published on a wide range of issues covering trade policy, development, the competitiveness of nations, the new economy and corporate governance.

Centre for European Policy Studies
Place du Congrès 1, B-1000 Brussels
Tel: 32 (0) 2 229.39.11 Fax: 32 (0) 2 219.41.51
e-mail: info@ceps.be
internet: http://www.ceps.be

CONTENTS

1. Introduction

The trade policy of the European Union is facing tremendous challenges. In 1995 the founding of the World Trade Organisation (WTO) was widely considered a milestone for world trade policy. Yet not long after its inception, the WTO's multilateral liberalisation has begun to slow down. One contributing factor is that, over the past few years, regional and bilateral trade agreements have been mushrooming, prompting the query of whether the WTO is being sidelined.

The EU is heavily dependant on open markets. Thus, enhanced access to third countries is an important element for growth and more jobs. This situation makes the question of which long-term trade policy strategy the EU should follow a key issue for European competitiveness. Should the EU give top priority to the WTO, rely on both multilateral and bilateral liberalisation or should it mainly pursue bilateral and regional agreements? These questions cannot be answered without an in-depth theoretical and empirical analysis of the trade policy options the EU has at its disposal. This study provides such an analysis and makes recommendations for EU trade policy.

Despite the EU's commitment to the multilateral system, the negotiations within the WTO are dragging on. To a large extent, this is caused by an intensified clash of interests between industrial and developing nations. Today, poorer countries represent the majority of WTO member states, and further, they are acting in a more self-confident manner. Therefore, it is becoming increasingly difficult to achieve agreement within the WTO framework, which requires unanimity. The fundamental conflicts have twice culminated in a collapse of WTO ministerial conferences, in Seattle in 1999 as well as in Cancun in 2003. Of course, the ongoing Doha Development Round that began in 2001 overcame a major obstacle in mid-2004, but further negotiations can be expected to remain sluggish and to achieve rather modest results. The EU is an important and constructive player within the WTO context. But there is no guarantee that its own constructive stance and concessions will drive the negotiations forward.

By contrast, there is strong momentum driving the conclusion of regional trade agreements. The most remarkable regional association is the EU itself. But the NAFTA in North America or ASEAN in Asia are also well known and are increasingly important. Approximately 50% of the 200 agreements that were in force in mid-2004 and reported to the WTO were concluded after 1995. Japan is representative of this trend. The country exclusively relied on the multilateral trade order up to a certain point, but not long ago underwent a paradigm shift and is now actively promoting the expansion of its bilateral trade agreements. Also, the US discerns a need to catch up with the EU[1] (which had already concluded many alliances predominantly with neighbouring countries) and is now increasingly playing the regional – and in particular the bilateral – card.

With the launch of the Doha Round of multilateral negotiations in 2001, the EU adopted the so-called 'Lamy doctrine': the highest priority is given to the WTO negotiations and these are complemented with a moratorium on entering new negotiations on bilateral deals. The longer the Doha Round is dragging on and the more regional integration proliferates around the world, the more urgent it becomes to question the risks associated with such a strategy.

What effects will the growing regionalisation have on EU competitiveness? Do EU companies run the risk of losing their competitive edge in the dynamic emerging markets in Asia? Is there perhaps a danger of large trade blocs forming that face each other in a hostile and protectionist manner (Sapir, 2000)? Does the intensive activity in concluding a large number of bilateral trade agreements pose a distraction from the multilateral approach? In order to answer these questions, a thorough analysis of the implications of regionalism is required.

Chapter 2 begins by examining the current status and the development of regional trade agreements, particularly bilateral ones. The discussion reveals the way in which the current phase of regionalism sets itself apart from earlier phases. Chapter 3 assesses the advantages and

---

[1] Strictly speaking, one would have to refer to the European Communities (EC), because the EC is the actor in the context of trade policy. Nevertheless, the term 'EU' is used throughout this study.

disadvantages of this development. In order to evaluate them, first the variety of motives for regional trade agreements are identified from the point of view of an individual country, and then which of these motives represent important determinants for the current phase of regionalism. The focus then shifts to a detailed study of the theoretical and empirical welfare effects of regional trade agreements as discussed in academic literature. The study next examines the question of whether the multitude of regional trade initiatives interferes with or promotes the multilateral dynamics of liberalisation. Finally, there is a discussion of whether the developing countries belong to the winners or losers of regionalism, and what opportunities regional associations offer with respect to new trade issues such as investment and competition.

On the basis of these findings, chapter 4 examines the EU's policy options from the perspective of self-interest. To this end, the specific options that are available to the EU are studied and evaluated. Alongside multilateral and bilateral liberalisation, it is possible to proceed either unilaterally or in larger groups (plurilaterally), in which case one must differentiate between the traditional dismantling of tariffs and new trade issues. The study also explores the responsibilities the EU should assume from a more general view of global trade policy. Based on these considerations, chapter 4 derives specific recommendations for EU trade policy. Chapter 5 summarises the results of the study.

2. Definitions and Status Quo

In international trade policy, 'regionalism' is used to refer to economic integration between two or more countries based on formal agreements (Siebert, 1997, p. 161; WTO, 2004; Kaiser, 2003, p. 25 et seq.). The trading partners concerned grant each other conditions that are preferential in comparison with other countries. In this context, the concept 'regional' refers to a limited number of countries and is used to set it apart from multilateral liberalisation, which includes all member states of the WTO. At the same time, this also means that non-members of the agreements are placed at a disadvantage with respect to members. Further, regionalism does not necessarily refer to unions of countries in specific regions (for instance, in Western Europe or in North America), although this is often the case, but also to trade agreements among countries on different continents.

Different levels of integration can be distinguished: [1]

- In a *preferential trade zone,* countries do not entirely abolish trade barriers *vis-à-vis* their partner countries. Essential product groups can also be excluded from trade liberalisation. Many agreements among developing countries belong in this category.

- By contrast, in a *free trade area,* internal tariffs and quantitative trade barriers such as import quotas are completely or almost totally abolished (for example, in the EU–South Africa case).

- This step also applies to *customs unions,* in which member countries additionally align their external tariffs with respect to third-party countries (as with the EU–Turkey example).

---

[1] See Siebert (1997, p. 199 et seq.), Kaiser (2003, p. 28 et seq.) and von Carlowitz (2003, p. 22 et seq.).

- With *common economic areas*, rules and technical standards are partially aligned (as in the European Economic Area, comprising the EU, Norway, Iceland and Liechtenstein).

- A *common market* means that not only goods, but also the production factors of labour and capital can move freely across internal borders. A certain degree of coordination of economic policy, for instance regarding financial or competition policy, is required (as seen in the concept of the EU internal market).

- In a *monetary union*, monetary and exchange rate policy is harmonised; in addition, an *economic union* standardises elements of economic policy with the objective of creating a uniform domestic market (such as the EU and particularly the EMU).

- Finally, in a *political union*, the competence for political decision-making is to a great extent centralised at the supranational level.

In practice, however, elements of these different integration levels often intermingle. Thus, a free trade area within narrow limits may exclude certain product groups (for example, agriculture) from liberalisation; but in other areas, it may go beyond the pure dismantling of tariffs, for instance regarding harmonisation of specific product standards, services or investment. It should be noted that liberalisation can take 10 years or more. Now and again, problems in implementation appear. In some cases, trade barriers are not lowered as planned and are sometimes even raised again.

Regional trade agreements – used here as a general term for different integration levels[2] – are seen to carry substantial weight in international trade policy. On 1 May 2004, 208 regional trade agreements were in force and registered with the WTO.[3] This figure does not yet include the enlargement of the EU. On top of this, approximately 60 to 80 additional agreements have been concluded, but are not yet registered with the WTO, a further 60 are in the negotiations phase and at least 30 more have been suggested (Schott, 2003; WTO, 2003a). Yet, these figures may not simply be summed up, because some regional trade agreements may render earlier agreements obsolete. For instance, EU enlargement has invalidated more than 60 agreements. Therefore, as of 18 November 2004, the WTO reports only 150 regional trade agreements. The following discussions in this study

---

[2] For brevity, occasionally the terms 'associations' or 'agreements' are used.

[3] Out of 124 agreements reported by 1995, only 48 are still in force.

are based on WTO data from May 2004, since the large number of agreements that in the meantime have become obsolete substantially characterised the overall situation, in particular with regard to Europe since the 1990s. This way, Europe's strong role as a pioneer of the new phase of regionalisation since the beginning of the 1990s remains visible.

All WTO member states with the exception of Mongolia are involved in at least one regional trade agreement. The WTO estimates that in 2005, approximately half of global trade has taken place within such associations (WTO, 2003b, p. 51). A series of important regional trade agreements and the relevance of these groupings' intra-exports for global trade are shown in Table 2.1, although it should be borne in mind that individual countries can be a member of more than one association.

Arranged by type of integration, two out of three reported associations represent free trade agreements concerning goods (66%) and 15% concern service agreements. The remaining nearly 20% are more or less evenly spread across customs unions, preferential agreements among developing countries and accessions to existing agreements.

With a view to the number of countries involved in the reported associations, bilateral agreements (preferential agreements, free trade agreements or service agreements) clearly form the overwhelming majority, with a share of around 80% of reported agreements. Most of these trade zones lie in Europe and Central Asia. Among the associations that are still in negotiation or have been suggested, the share of bilateral agreements is higher still. Plurilateral agreements between more than two countries represent a share of only about 13% of the agreements reported by May 2004.[4]

The strong increase of regional agreements since the middle of the 1990s is particularly noteworthy. Between 1995 and May 2004, about 50% of these agreements came into force, although this period represents less than one-fifth of the time since 1948 (see Figure 2.1).[5]

---

[4] Four plurilateral service agreements that were concluded in addition to existing agreements concerning trade in goods are not included here.

[5] This figure also includes earlier agreements that are no longer in force. If one considers only those agreements that are still in force, this figure is about 70%. These specifications are qualified to a certain extent by the fact that WTO membership and reporting obligations have increased since the mid-1990s (WTO, 2003a).

Table 2.1 Selected regional trade agreements (in 2002)

Abbreviation	Name	Share of trade bloc's exports of world exports (in %)	Share of intra-exports of trade bloc's entire exports (in %)
EU-15	European Union – 15 member states	37.9	60.6
NAFTA	North American Free Trade Area	17.2	56.7
Andean	Andean Group	0.8	9.5
CACM	Central American Common Market	0.4	11.1
CARICOM	Caribbean Community and Common Market	0.2	12.5
MERCOSUR	Southern Cone Common Market (Mercado Común del Sur)	1.4	11.6
CEMAC	Economic and Monetary Community of Central Africa	0.1	1.5
COMESA	Common Market for Eastern and Southern Africa	0.4	6.4
SADC	South Africa Development Community	0.7	9.3
UEMOA	West African Economic and Monetary Union	0.1	12.3
ASEAN	Association of South-East Asian Nations	6.3	23.7

Notes: EU – Austria, Belgium, Denmark, Finland, France, Germany, Greece, Ireland, Italy, Luxembourg, Netherlands, Portugal, Spain, Sweden, the UK

NAFTA – Canada, Mexico, the US

Andean Group – Bolivia, Colombia, Ecuador, Peru, Venezuela

CACM – Costa Rica, El Salvador, Guatemala, Honduras, Nicaragua

CARICOM – Antigua, Barbuda, the Bahamas, Barbados, Belize, Dominica, Grenada, Guyana, Jamaica, Montserrat, Saint Kitts and Nevis, Saint Lucia, Saint Vincent and the Grenadines, Suriname, Trinidad, Tobago

MERCOSUR – Argentina, Brazil, Paraguay, Uruguay

CEMAC – Cameroon, the Central African Republic, Chad, Republic of the Congo, Rwanda

COMESA – Angola, Burundi, Comoros, Democratic Republic of the Congo, Djibouti, Egypt, Eritrea, Ethiopia, Kenya, Madagascar, Malawi, Mauritius, Namibia, Rwanda, the Seychelles, Sudan, Swaziland, Uganda, Tanzania, Zambia

SADC – Angola, Botswana, Democratic Republic of the Congo, Lesotho, Malawi, Mauritius, Mozambique, Namibia, Seychelles, South Africa, Swaziland, Tanzania, Zambia, Zimbabwe

UEMOA – Benin, Burkina Faso, the Ivory Coast, Guinea-Bissau, Mali, Niger, Senegal, Togo

ASEAN – Brunei Darussalam, Cambodia, Indonesia, People's Democratic Republic of Laos, Malaysia, Myanmar, the Philippines, Singapore, Thailand, Vietnam

Source: World Bank (2004, pp. 318-320).

Figure 2.1 Reported regional trade agreements that are in force, by year of coming into force – Annual averages

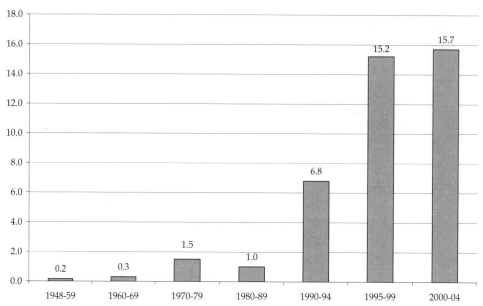

Notes: Status as of 1 May 2004; the data shown still contain all trade agreements by the EU accession countries that have lapsed owing to the EU's eastern enlargement. If these are not taken into consideration, the number of the reported regional trade agreements that are in force decreases from 208 to 150 (as of 18 November 2004). For the 1990-94 period, the annual average referred to here decreases to 4.6, and to 6.6 for the 1995-99 period.

Sources: WTO (retrieved from www.wto.org/english/tratop_e/region_e/regfac_e.htm, 23 May and 28 November 2004) and authors' calculations.

Initially, after European integration in the 1960s and 1970s, the first smaller wave of trade agreements occurred mainly among developing countries, but they generally did not achieve their sometimes ambitious objectives (which included economic and monetary unions) or remained unimportant (Krueger, 1999; Kaiser, 2003, p. 45 et seq.). In the 1980s, the activity then abated noticeably, before rising to hitherto unknown levels during the 1990s.

In qualitative terms, an old and a new wave[6] of regional integration can be distinguished over the last several decades as discussed below: [7]

- Nine out of ten of the reported agreements between 1995 and May 2004 were bilateral in nature, while of those associations that were in force prior to 1985, only around half were concluded between just two countries. In recent times, the first bilateral agreements have begun to emerge between plurilateral associations (for example, the EC–MERCOSUR (still under negotiation) and the CARICOM–CACM agreements).

- The associations that include developing countries are less characterised by protectionism and policies of import substitution than in the past. Rather, numerous developing countries use North-South agreements to better secure (lock-in) their reforms of international trade and partly bolster their general economic policy (see chapter 3, section 3.5).

- No longer is trade in goods alone covered in the striving towards traditional, step-by-step integration beyond a free trade area up to a customs union and beyond. Increasingly, they also include issues such as services, investment, competition, standards or environmental and social norms.[8]

- The number of active individual participants that are spinning a web of bilateral agreements has risen sharply; figuratively speaking, they are becoming hubs surrounded by spokes. Since the mid-1990s, more

---

[6] Here the use of the word 'new' is to be understood in a broader and less conceptual sense than in the term 'New Regionalism' coined by Ethier (1998). As an advocate of regional trade agreements, Ethier views regionalism as the result of the multilateral liberalisation of trade, which leads to a strengthening of trade integration among countries that are near each other geographically. Associations among these countries would lead to fewer trade diversion problems (see chapter 3, section 3.2) and agreements between industrial and developing countries in particular should tend to have additional advantages.

[7] On this point, see Ethier (1998), Krueger (1999), Langhammer & Wößmann (2002), Lloyd (2002), Kaiser (2003, p. 29 et seq.), WTO (2003a) and Schiff & Winters (2003, p. 1 et seq.).

[8] In this context, the World Bank (World Bank, 2004, p. 35) provides a fairly comprehensive overview regarding important regional trade agreements.

and more countries have pursued this aim and have considerably strengthened their activities during the current decade.[9]

   o   Primarily, this includes the US (Hilaire & Yang, 2003; Schott, 2004). After they had previously followed the multilateral path exclusively and had actively promoted it, they joined their first bilateral associations in the 1980s and the early 1990s. They did this without an explicit strategy and rather reactively (Feinberg, 2003). Since the Trade Promotion Authority was passed by Congress in 2002, however, in parallel to the new round of global trade negotiations the US administration has energetically focused on the conclusion of bilateral trade agreements with countries in Africa, the Middle and the Far East. They are also pursuing this strategy on the American continent (including the Caribbean), but with the medium-term objective of establishing a Pan-American free trade zone (Free Trade Area of the Americas or FTAA). All of this has been embedded in a strategy of 'competitive liberalisation', whereby multilateral, regional and bilateral negotiations should compete with and reinforce each other (USTR, 2004).

   o   In addition, a number of emerging countries such as Mexico, Chile, Singapore, South Korea and Thailand are surrounding themselves with a network of bilateral contracts.

   o   In Eastern Asia, for some years there has also been lively activity regarding the conclusion, and above all, the planning of bilateral associations (Lloyd, 2002). ASEAN is especially trying to become a hub in the area by announcing several bilateral associations with Australia, New Zealand, South Korea, Japan, India and China. It is noteworthy that until the late 1990s, Asia (including Japan, Australia and New Zealand) largely subscribed to a multilateral strategy, but is now giving the impression that it intends to rapidly catch up in concluding bilateral associations (for further examples, see Lloyd & MacLaren, 2003 and Dieter, 2003, p. 14 et seq.).

---

[9] The large number of associations among former Eastern bloc countries can barely be considered to constitute new regionalism, given that earlier trade agreements within the scope of COMECON were replaced.

    o   Until the 1980s, the European Communities (and the European Free Trade Area or EFTA) were forerunners of bilateral associations. After the fall of the iron curtain, this trend intensified. The EU concluded numerous bilateral agreements with Central and Eastern European countries as well as with Turkey (a customs union), which in the majority of cases led to or will lead to EU accession. In the second half of the 1990s and beyond, this trend continued, for example leading to agreements with Mexico, Chile and South Africa. In addition, the majority of the remaining south-eastern European countries were and will be included to the same extent as the Mediterranean countries of Northern Africa and the Middle East, with whom mostly bilateral trade agreements have existed for some time, albeit less comprehensively. After all, the EU also wants to develop the one-sided preferences *vis-à-vis* the African, Caribbean and Pacific (ACP) countries into reciprocal bilateral agreements. It is remarkable, however, that the EU announced a moratorium at the beginning of this decade (and of the new world trade round), and has since taken up no more new negotiations. Those association negotiations that had been decided upon previously are being continued (for instance with MERCOSUR). But after the conclusion of the Doha Round, EU Trade Commissioner Peter Mandelson has already signalled that he is not likely to disfavour new bilateral associations.

- The result is an increasingly complicated network of often overlapping associations ('spaghetti bowl phenomenon').
- A certain tendency can be discerned towards forming regional blocs: in Europe with EU enlargement and the connections with the EFTA and numerous Mediterranean countries; in America with the planned Pan-American FTAA; in Asia with the activities of ASEAN and other countries in the region; in the Middle East the pan-Arabian free trade zone (planned by 2007); and in Africa with an as yet rather vague African economic community (WTO, 2003a). The EU for instance promotes this tendency among the ACP countries by preferring to negotiate with countries that have previously formed regional trade agreements.

- Indeed, regional integration on the respective continents is put into perspective by the fact that in recent times, associations are increasingly formed that span continents. This trend for instance includes agreements between the EU and Chile, Mexico or South Africa as well as those between the US and Singapore or Australia, or between South Korea and Chile. Furthermore, the Asian-Pacific region is connected by the – albeit rather ineffectual – Asian-Pacific Economic Cooperation (APEC). Yet associations between Western Europe and East Asia exist just as little nowadays as do associations between the US and Europe.[10] Currently, there is no sign that the trade blocs that are slowly developing confront each other in a hostile manner, a fear that is occasionally expressed by some researchers (Sapir, 2000). Rather, the integration of trade especially between the EU and the US (reinforced by close investment ties) as well as between East Asia and the US is so dense that such a protectionist scenario does not appear very likely.

- To some degree, a certain simplification occurs because individual agreements lapse, as can be seen for example in the EU's eastern enlargement or in the agreement between Mexico and CACM as an entire association, rather than (as before) an agreement between Mexico and every individual CACM member.

---

[10] The trade relations between the EU and the ACP countries as well as the non-reciprocal agreements between industrial and developing countries within the scope of the Generalised System of Preferences are not taken into account here.

3. Pros and Cons of Regionalism

The dynamic and diverse development of trade agreements raises the question of how the latest wave of regionalism and bilateralism should be assessed from an economic perspective. In the academic debate, however, there is no consensus (see for instance Matthes, 2001, pp. 27-31), because there is a range of potential advantages as well as numerous possible disadvantages whose relative weight can hardly be objectively assessed. Hence, it is not surprising that among eminent economists there are researchers who tend to be advocates of certain forms of regionalism (for example, Wilfried Ethier, Lawrence Summers, Robert Lawrence and Fred Bergsten) as well as opponents (such as Jagdish Bhagwati, Arvind Panagariya, Paul Krugman and Anne O. Krueger) who are more or less clearly against this tendency in global trade. In this chapter the pros and cons of regionalism presented by these and other economists are considered in greater detail and in different perspectives.

3.1 Causes of increased regionalism

A first question concerns the driving forces behind the dynamism in concluding regional trade agreements in recent times. In this section the basic motives for such associations are considered from the perspective of an individual country as stated in the literature.[1]

Starting with the non-economic reasons, first geopolitical and diplomatic motives should be mentioned, although they cannot necessarily be regarded as new as elaborated below:

---

[1] This section draws upon Baldwin (1997), Ethier (1998), Krueger (1999), Panagariya (1999), Schiff & Winters (2003, p. 6 et seq., p. 101 et seq. and p. 187 et seq.), WTO (2003b, p. 49 et seq.), Kaiser (2003, p. 152 et seq.), von Carlowitz (2003, p. 25 et seq. and p. 74 et seq.) and World Bank (2004, p. 35 et seq.).

- For the purposes of classical diplomacy, these agreements can represent instruments to intensify relations with certain countries in an entirely general sense, to promote political stability, to protect peace or possibly to fight terrorism and the cultivation of drugs. European integration up to the EU's eastern enlargement is an example of an association that is to a large extent politically motivated. Economic integration, through economic policy bodies, served to overcome former political antagonisms. Further, the recent US initiatives concerning bilateral agreements, mainly with countries in the Middle East or with some countries in Latin America in which drugs are cultivated, are at least partially politically motivated. The aim of peacekeeping is also mentioned in the context of MERCOSUR and ASEAN.

- The establishment of regional trade agreements can serve to enhance negotiating power (for example, MERCOSUR *vis-à-vis* the US or ASEAN *vis-à-vis* the larger trading partners in the Asian region). Nevertheless, it is worth noting that as a general rule regional associations at the multilateral level do not appear as a group, with the exception of the EU (for example, MERCOSUR, CACM and CARICOM).

- It is possible that – once established – a bureaucracy fears that it might be scaled down in the medium term if it is needed to a lesser degree for the purpose of multilateral negotiations. Regional trade agreements could then serve to provide added fields of activity and justification for their continued existence.

Additionally, there is a range of economic reasons for countries to conclude regional trade agreements.[2] Hidden protectionist intentions can play a role when access to the market of the partner country is improved to the advantage of one's own industry and at the expense of competition from outside the association. This approach played an important role in

---

[2] To the extent that the objective is to substitute ineffective domestic production with more efficient foreign production and to intensify competition domestically, unilateral or multilateral liberalisation is to be preferred to the regional approach. For a detailed analysis of the economic and welfare-theoretical effects of regional trade agreements, see section 3.2. This includes the motivation to use regionalism in order to improve the terms of trade at the expense of third countries.

many early agreements among developing countries. During the past few years protectionist tendencies have evidently faded into the background.

Anyhow, a regional trade agreement means that third countries are placed at a relative disadvantage. This prompts a defensive reaction to conclude regional trade agreements or to join them so as not to be excluded. On the basis of this idea, Richard E. Baldwin (1997) constructs his domino theory, according to which a new agreement or the extension of an existing agreement leads to added associations or accessions. As examples he primarily points to the consequent effect of the EU's Single Market programme in the form of accession requests by numerous countries that were members of European Free Trade Area (EFTA) at that time (among others, Austria, Sweden and Switzerland) as well as a number of agreements among Latin-American countries as a result of the rejection of their request for accession to the NAFTA (among others, MERCOSUR).[3]

On the basis of the realisation that regional agreements place non-members at a disadvantage, there are presently indications of a rivalry between the EU and the US regarding attractive markets for their respective export industries. The US has seen the need to catch up with the EU's large number of regional associations, and has likewise begun to weave a network of bilateral agreements with some markets that are important for them. By contrast, the EU has tried to not fall behind with respect to the US with emerging countries that are economically important such as Mexico, Chile and the MERCOSUR countries, and for that purpose

---

[3] The political-economic model of Baldwin has some weaknesses (von Carlowitz, 2003, p. 92 et seq.; Kaiser, 2003, p. 176 et seq.). For instance, it does not consider the possibility of a request for accession being refused. In addition, the assumption regarding the political-economic process in the rejected country have been called into question. In such a case, the export industry in the country – being put at a disadvantage by the association of other countries – is assumed to intensify its lobbying efforts in order to regain its market access. On the other hand, the import-substitution industry (which as a rule would be affected negatively by liberalisation) does not oppose this tendency in Baldwin's model, as one might expect. Cases are conceivable, however, in which Baldwin's assumption is not unrealistic. Such cases could include those where the partner of an industrial country is an emerging country with little influence on trade policy and which demands no equivalent quid pro quo by the industrial country; where vulnerable sectors are excluded from the outset (for example, agriculture); or where owing to an agreement, there is an increase in intensive intra-industrial trade export opportunities for an industry that competes with imports.

has been concluding associations that span continents. This development has for the time being slowed down owing to the EU moratorium previously noted. Nevertheless, in recent times it has become apparent that the EU might also conclude free trade agreements in the Asian region in order to avoid trade-diverting effects with respect to other emerging countries, but primarily to the US and Japan.

Most of the more recent regional trade agreements have been concluded between large industrialised countries as well as developing or emerging countries (or both) in their geographical neighbourhood. For the EU this concerns above all Central and Eastern Europe, but also the Mediterranean area; in the US, it primarily relates to Mexico, but also the Caribbean and other Latin American countries. From the perspective of the developing and emerging countries, this represents an attempt – which is not fundamentally new – to improve access to a large market that is of great importance to them (see section 3.5). This trend is also associated with the hope of protecting oneself against protectionist backlashes, for instance in the form of anti-dumping measures by important trading partners. For example, in 2002 Mexico was excluded from US safeguard duties on steel products, and within the EU anti-dumping-measures have been abolished among member countries. Often, by generally liberalising to a greater extent than the larger partner, developing countries pay a kind of premium for the protection of market access (for references, see Kaiser, 2003, p. 164 et seq.).[4]

New aspects in this development principally concern the effects of intensified globalisation on the incentive to conclude regional trade agreements among neighbouring industrialised and developing or emerging countries. Falling barriers to trade, lower communication costs and increasingly mobile capital, knowledge and technologies facilitate the fragmentation of production processes in different locations. From the perspective of the companies in industrialised countries, the opportunity thus lies at their doorstep to outsource labour-intensive processes and to realise considerable cost advantages. In this way, developing and emerging

---

[4] In addition, the industrial nations use their individual bargaining power, which is larger than that within the multilateral framework, to impose environmental and social standards as well as – in the case of the US – rules for the protection of intellectual property rights and a ban on restrictions on the movement of capital (Hilaire & Yang, 2003) (see section 3.5). This is a new development in that for the most part these issues have only arisen in the recent past.

countries benefit in the form of higher exports and increased economic growth. In addition, they attract more foreign direct investment from large neighbouring countries and hope to thereby noticeably improve their growth prospects. Mexico and the Eastern European EU-accession countries are prime examples of this.

The advantages of this strategy can be further increased if the smaller countries have adopted a free-market economic policy and thus improved the investment climate. Here another rather new aspect of regionalism comes into play. Such an about-turn in reform policy is a phenomenon of the later 1980s and especially the 1990s. In this regard, regional trade agreements can have an additional advantage for developing countries. Such an about-turn only leads to more economic activity if it is credible. Yet in those countries in which reforms were in the past conducted half-heartedly or were even rescinded, politics lack credibility. In such countries, a regional trade agreement can lock-in reforms and can act as a positive outward signal. Therefore, revoking trade liberalisation – which in the case of unilateral liberalisation is possible at any time without penalty – carries with it the threat of counter-reaction on the part of the trading partner. Nevertheless, this advantage of regional trade agreements is subject to a number of restrictions (see section 3.5).

Developing and emerging countries have also used bilateral agreements over the past years to reduce their dependence on large neighbouring markets. For instance, this applies to the agreements concluded by Chile and Mexico with some Asian countries and the EU.

Another important motive for regional trade agreements that in recent times has gained prominence is the sluggish liberalisation negotiations within the WTO framework.[5] One major disadvantage of the

---

[5] This often-mentioned criticism can be connected to a contribution by Andrew Rose (2002 and 2004). Rose argues that it cannot be statistically proven that WTO members have a more liberal trade policy or significantly different trade patterns than non-WTO members. In response, Subramanian & Wei (2003) pin down this seemingly disappointing result to the history of the GATT negotiations, which up to the Uruguay Round involved significant trade liberalisation in merchandise basically by industrial countries alone and even then excluded sectors such as agriculture as well as textiles and clothing. While this can, of course, be seen as disappointing, it is obvious that industrial countries have lowered tariffs in industrial goods trade immensely (see chapter 4, Table 4.1). Moreover, the introduction of developing countries as well as agriculture, textiles and clothing

multilateral level that is often cited is that, above all, the costs of forging a consensus on liberalisation are very high owing to the large number of members. Hence it is said that the conclusions of such agreements take longer and are less extensive (see for example, Ethier, 1998). These objections can be qualified, however, if one looks at the experiences of earlier negotiation rounds and multilateral achievements to date:

- The argument concerning the large number of members can be called into question, because in the end, it depends on the number of politically active members. Up to the last (Uruguay) trade round, progress in the WTO negotiations depended on a few decisive actors (among others the US, the EU, exporters of agricultural goods and important emerging countries).[6] A large number of developing countries have behaved passively and accepted the agreements negotiated among the large partners.

- A wide range of new subjects has opened up for discussion within the WTO framework, such as services, intellectual property and subsidies as well as rudimentary rules for investments relevant to trade. These new topics complicate negotiations but make them more important in economic terms.

- Further, it was the EU that delayed progress in negotiations during the Uruguay Round because it refused to reduce the protectionism of its agricultural sector – which is not necessarily the fault of the multilateral system.

- In past rounds, negotiations took place in short, but mostly intensive stages. Long periods with seemingly no progress in negotiations are not new.

- The argument that with regional trade agreements one is pursuing a faster and easier path than within the WTO framework does not generally apply, because regional trade agreements have in some

---

and services into the international trading order in the course of the Uruguay Round can be seen as a significant step forward. Although the liberalisation in services and to some extent in agricultural trade has not been very pronounced (on which more will hopefully be achieved in the Doha Round), the elimination of the quota system for textiles and clothing represents a major success.

[6] There is, however, a positive correlation between the number of WTO members and the duration of the negotiation rounds (Neary, 2004), which of course still says nothing about causality.

cases also taken a long time to negotiate, as seen in the process of European integration or the Free Trade Area of the Americas (FTAA), which initially entered discussions at the beginning of the 1990s. The tough negotiations between the EU and MERCOSUR, which have been hampered by setbacks, are another current example.

The question still arises as to whether the current problems of the Doha Round are comparable with the problems of earlier rounds. For instance, the number of members has grown considerably since the end of the Uruguay Round – up to 148 states. The numeric dominance of the developing countries has therefore grown substantially (Figure 3.1).

Figure 3.1 Number of WTO members

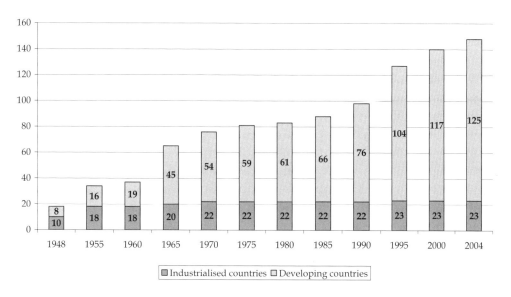

Note: Until 1994, these were the contracting parties to the GATT.

Sources: WTO (retrieved from http://www.wto.org/english/thewto_e/whatis_e/tif_e/org6_e.htm, 23 November 2004) and authors' calculations.

Above all, however, the developing countries – including the poorest among them – have become far more active. Indeed, in Cancun in 2003 they united to form various groups, a tactic that reduces the costs of negotiation and conclusion. Yet the heterogeneity of interests is significant, so that the chances of reaching agreements have rather diminished. For instance, a large number of poorer developing countries view multilateral liberalisation critically because up to now they have been enjoying preferential access to the markets of important industrialised countries – a benefit that would depreciate in value by an overall reduction of barriers to trade (erosion of preferences).

Another motive for concluding or threatening to conclude regional trade agreements can be to exert pressure on the negotiating partners at the multilateral level. For instance, the establishment of NAFTA or APEC in the early 1990s is also seen in this context.[7] In the aftermath of the failed Cancun conference, threats by the US and the EU to enter into associations with selected countries (which would not take into account many underdeveloped countries) belong in this category.

3.2 Welfare analysis

Theoretical analysis

These and other rather political motives for regional trade agreements raise the question of how sensible such a strategy really is from an economic point of view when considered in greater detail. Such behaviour should be compared with liberalisation, which leads to free trade without discrimination. Unilateral or multilateral reduction in trade barriers are the suitable methods for this to happen. With free trade, the efficiency of the international division of labour is maximised, since every country specialises in accordance with its comparative cost advantages. Additional advantages arise from a broader choice of goods, a higher competitive intensity, the use of economies of scale in production and possible technological spillover effects conducive to growth. Therefore, from the point of view of an individual country, it is in theory advantageous to unilaterally liberalise markets.[8] Tariffs and other barriers to trade mean that

---

[7] This strategy is discussed in greater detail in section 3.4.

[8] For a detailed theoretical and empirical analysis of the gains-from-trade proposition as well as for some theoretically derivable exceptions see Matthes (2004). Nevertheless, politically, unilateral liberalisation is often hard to enforce because the usually well-organised import-substitution industry opposes this step in the political process, while on the other hand, the interests of the consumers are difficult to organise. With multilateral liberalisation, there is the promise of improved access to export markets, so that the export industry can form a counterbalance to the interests of the import-substitution industry (see also chapter 4, section 4.2). If the national labour market is not sufficiently adaptable to create

consumers pay prices that are too high and efficiency losses occur because the advantages in the form of customs revenue (or import quota rent) and higher profits for the import-substitution industry do not offset the losses suffered by the consumers. Further, increasing competitive pressure leads domestic companies to produce more efficiently, to become more innovative and to focus more on customer's needs.

With regional trade agreements, the theoretical analysis from the perspective of an individual country is considerably more differentiated and will therefore be summarised in the following discussion.[9] Most studies only assume – within the scope of a partial equilibrium analysis – the market of an economically small country A. Initially, country A levies identical duties with respect to two countries, B and C and on a good that is produced under perfectly competitive conditions and with constant returns to scale, so that costs increase in proportion to output quantity. This leads to a rising supply function for A (S_A) (Figure 3.2). The countries B and C are, however, large countries in comparison to A. Hence, the export quantities on the market in A (or the demand by A) are not of great significance to B or C. Costs do not increase, and their supply functions are horizontal with respect to the market in A (without duties S_B, S_C, with duties S_{Bt}, S_{Ct}). The shape of the cost curves in Figure 3.2 is chosen such that at low output quantities A can export at a lower price than B and C. But at higher output quantities, A becomes more expensive than B and C. By assumption, B offers a higher price than C, whereby the cost difference is smaller than the duty levied by country A. In addition, even including duties, country C is cheaper than A at higher output quantities.[10]

---

new employment opportunities for employees who are released in the course of the structural change that is induced by liberalisation, it may be sensible to lower trade barriers not in one go, but rather gradually.

[9] Early studies about this question primarily comprise the fundamental work of Viner (1950) as well as extensions of the analysis by for instance Meade (1955), Lipsey (1960) and Corden (1972). More current overviews of the underlying theory are presented for example by Baldwin & Venables (1995), Siebert (1997, p. 202 et seq.), Rose & Sauernheimer (1999, p. 627 et seq.), Panagariya (2000) as well as in Zimmermann (1999, p. 8 et seq.), von Carlowitz (2003, p. 26 et seq. and p. 100 et seq.) Kaiser (2003, p. 72 et seq.) and Baldwin & Wyplosz (2004, Part II).

[10] The following reflections are also valid for appropriate characteristics of the supply function if in comparison with A, countries B and C are not economically large countries, and thus the supply functions of B and C likewise increase.

Figure 3.2 Consequences of a customs union between countries A and B

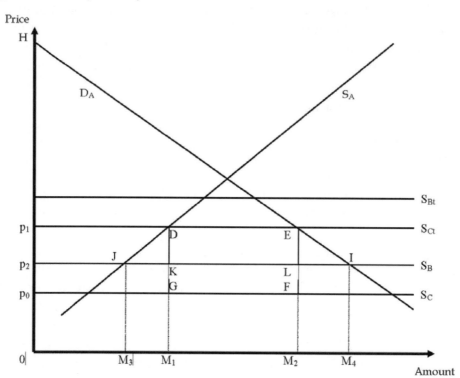

Sources: Author's illustration in accordance with Siebert (1997, p. 202) and Rose & Sauernheimer (1999, p. 629).

Initially, A levies an equally high tariff rate t on exports from B and C amounting to the difference between p_1 and p_0. Country A produces the amount of 0-M_1 itself and imports from C the amount of M_1M_2 at price p_1. In doing so, customs revenue is incurred in the amount of M_1M_2 multiplied with tariff rate t (rectangle DEFG).

If A eliminates tariffs with respect to B and enters into a customs union with B, then B can offer its goods at an 'artificially' lower price than C. Supply function S_B now applies to B. As a result, within A, the price of the good falls from p_1 to p_2. Two effects can be distinguished:

- On the one hand, trade is created because a share of A's production is substituted with cheaper production from B (M_3M_1) and also, on account of the lower price, demand increases (M_2M_4). Thus total imports from A rise by $M_3M_1 + M_2M_4$. These effects raise A's welfare.

- On the other hand, trade is diverted in the amount of M_1M_2 because A is no longer importing this amount from the cheapest country C, but from the relatively more expensive country B. This effect decreases A's welfare.

Both effects must be netted against each other in order to determine whether the customs union improves welfare for country A. The effects on welfare can be graphically illustrated as follows:

- The consumers in A benefit from lower prices and consume more (M_2M_4). Consumer surplus (and welfare) thus increases by p_1EIp_2.[11]
- This is counter-balanced by two negative welfare effects –
  - The profits of domestic producers in country A fall by p_1DJp_2, because they can sell less (by the amount represented by M_3M_1).[12]
  - Further, customs revenue is entirely lost (DEFG), which also reduces welfare if one assumes that the government would originally have distributed this income as a per capita lump sum.

Consequently, the net effect on welfare stems from balancing these effects represented by the areas mentioned. Of the consumer surplus, triangles DKJ and EIL in Figure 3.2 represent the increase in welfare – and the area KLFG represents the welfare loss as a result of reduced customs revenue. The latter area reflects diversion of trade, because A must now make purchases more expensively in B than it could otherwise have made in C (without tariffs). If in this simple illustration the negative effects of trade diversion outbalance the positive effects of the generation of trade, a customs union reduces welfare in country A. Otherwise, welfare increases.

---

[11] This effect can be split: On the one hand, those consumers for which the good is worth less than p1 (but more than p2) will now also buy the good, represented by the triangle EIL. On the other hand, the remaining consumers now pay less than before (rectangle p1ELp2).

[12] Regarding the output quantity M1, this effect can also be interpreted as follows: as now only p2 must be paid for the same amount instead of p1, the consumer surplus increases by p1DKp2. Producers' profits decline, however, by the amount of p1DJp2. The balance of welfare is positive, in the amount of DKJ. This result reflects that this share of production in country A was previously inefficient and therefore wasted resources.

Because effects on welfare can barely be measured in practice, one could assume that one might offset the increased import amount in A with displaced exports coming from C. If the balance is positive – according to this train of thought – the balance of creation and diversion of trade would also have to be positive. Yet, it is not sufficient to only balance trade volumes, since differences in costs also play a role. Thus, the positive effect of trade creation is greater, the larger the cost difference is between A and B; the magnitude of the negative effect depends on the cost differences between B and C. *A priori*, no unequivocal statement is possible.

To be sure, there is still a whole range of additional aspects to be considered if the effects on welfare are to be extensively analysed. It becomes clear that even with a negative balance of the previous effects, a positive effect on welfare is possible, but not certain:

- If several goods are taken into account, a customs union also leads to shifts in consumption patterns by changing relative prices. This effect can diminish or reinforce distortions in the consumption structure that are detrimental to welfare. The direction of the effect depends on many factors and cannot be determined unambiguously in advance.

- If A is a large country, its supply and demand influence prices abroad. The lowering of tariffs with respect to B increases demand in country A for goods imported from B, and also increases A's import prices relative to A's export prices. Therefore, country A must export more to be able to afford the same amount of imports – this means the so-called (internal) 'terms of trade' have become worse. But at the same time, B also lowers its tariffs. If B is large enough and this has an effect on prices in country A, in turn A identically benefits from this step because its terms of trade improve. Generally, in the case of countries of more or less equal size, *ceteris paribus* the country with previously higher tariffs should tend to experience a welfare loss.

- If the customs union is large with respect to country C and can therefore affect prices there, the welfare of the customs union will increase. Since the (external) terms of trade *vis-à-vis* C improve ,because by diversion of trade there, the demand for goods exported from C decreases, C's export prices fall in relation to its import prices. This effect is even reinforced if, in addition, exports from A or B to C are diverted towards the customs union, because then the imported amounts are reduced in country C and C's import prices increase in relation to C's export prices.

If the assumption of perfect competition is given up, and increasing returns to scale are permitted (falling average costs for instance owing to high fixed costs), additional effects on welfare arise.

- By the abolition of tariffs, the manufacturers that benefit (from the creation and diversion of trade) in the customs union can serve a larger market. Their production quantity increases and average costs fall. Consequently, fewer resources must be employed per unit of production, which increases welfare.[13] Positive effects can be elevated further. As far as A's imported good is now produced in country B at a better price than in C (without tariffs) through advantages of scale, from A's perspective this no longer results in a diversion of trade, because the good is now purchased from B, the most cost-efficient supplier.[14] In this case, the previous import of this good by B from country C is also curbed, additionally increasing production in B. An identical effect is achieved by a probable, total displacement of suppliers in A by suppliers in B – thus, trade creation is increased.

- Liberalisation further results in an expanded range of goods, which in turn augments welfare.

- The competitive intensity grows with respect to the partner country because of liberalisation.[15] This outcome has several welfare-increasing effects. On the one hand, in formerly narrow markets, there is a reduction in the monopoly or oligopoly profits that originated from the fact that output was lower and prices higher than in the case of perfect competition. Additionally, the companies have greater incentives to produce more cost-effectively and to develop innovations. Moreover, industrial restructuring leads to fewer, but larger firms, which implies a larger production scale. All these effects reduce costs and tend to diminish trade-diverting effects.

---

[13] As an indirect effect of the price reduction, demand slightly increases again. Subsequently, production increases once more and average costs continue to fall.

[14] Yet this only applies if countries B and C exhibit the same conditions of production. Should C have comparative cost advantages and hence (at the same production level) can produce at a better price, diversion of trade will occur.

[15] Strictly speaking, this applies only to the import-substitution industry, because for A's export industry the conditions of access in country B improve and thus competitive pressure tends to be reduced. Until now, this aspect has hardly been addressed in the academic literature (Baldwin & Venables, 1995).

- Owing to increased innovation and the possible technological spillover effects that can originate from trade or increased foreign direct investment, growth can rise within the customs union, thereby additionally increasing welfare (see Matthes, 2004, chapter 3.2).

Most of these additional effects of regional integration tend to enhance welfare beyond the results of simply comparing the creation and diversion of trade. From the theoretical perspective, however, a positive net effect is not guaranteed.

Against this background, it is interesting to examine which economic factors influence regional trade agreements. The results of an econometric analysis (Baier & Bergstrand, 2004) show that trade agreements between two countries are more likely to lead to welfare gains for the countries involved and thus become more likely, [16]

- the lower the geographical distance is between both trading partners and the greater the distance is to the non-members;
- the larger and the more similar the countries are economically, reinforcing the exploitation of advantages of scale in producing differentiated products and favouring the creation of intra-industrial trade;
- the greater the differences are in the comparative advantages between both countries, so that strong opportunities for specialisation and trade exist and thereby a large potential for inter-industrial trade; and
- the smaller the differences are in the comparative advantages between the pair of countries and the non-members, limiting the magnitude of trade diversion.

Nevertheless, it should be taken into account that from the perspective of an individual country, a situation with tariffs has been compared with a situation involving a discriminatory dismantling of tariffs. If unilateral or multilateral liberalisation is considered, some of the positive welfare effects indicated above are put into perspective in cases where the most efficient supplier is situated outside the customs union. If average costs fall through increasing returns to scale, welfare gains in country A are

---

[16] On the basis of 1,431 country pairs from which 286 were involved in a regional trade agreement (in 1996), the econometric model correctly forecasts 243 (or 85%) of these associations.

larger if the more efficient supplier in C increases production instead of the artificially preferred supplier in B. In this scenario, the choice of products might also be wider than in the case of regional liberalisation. Furthermore, the competitive intensity rises more strongly if the most efficient suppliers have equal market access. Specialisation is also prevented in sectors in which there are no comparative cost advantages, which would damage growth in the long term.

From a global perspective, this point is of key importance since global resources are only used efficiently if every country is in a position to specialise in its comparative cost advantages and no distortion of market access exists among individual countries.

In addition, not only is the welfare of the customs union to be considered from a global perspective, but also that of third countries, which one could consider to represent the rest of the world. This study has so far pointed out how country C suffers disadvantages in various ways by potentially-induced trade diversion:

- As far as the demand for export goods from country C decreases and this leads to price effects in C, producers' profits fall in C and the terms of trade deteriorate.[17]

- The same applies if the supply of import goods in C from the customs union declines, thereby raising prices in C. The consumers there are also placed at a disadvantage.

- In addition, in the case of increasing returns to scale, a decline in the demand for exports represents an increase in costs, because production falls and average costs rise accordingly. More resources must be employed for the production of the goods concerned.

- Further, the choice of goods in country C would tend to be reduced.

Yet these disadvantages must be viewed in contrast to possible advantages of the customs union from the perspective of country C. Thus, effects on the structure of consumption can have a positive (as well as a negative) effect on welfare. But above all, C should profit from higher macroeconomic demand by the customs union, because income and growth should increase as a result of the customs union. Again, the balance of these effects cannot be determined unambiguously.

---

[17] If several third countries are taken into consideration, the possibility cannot be discounted that in specific countries terms of trade improve.

All in all, the establishment of a customs union – as indicated earlier in the context of the simple model – should be more likely to result in positive welfare effects for the countries involved as well as for the world in total, the more trade is created and the less it is diverted. For these conditions, some general requirements can be derived:[18]

The creation of trade will be larger,

- the higher the tariffs between countries A and B were in the original situation;

- the larger the cost differences are between country A and country B; and

- the stronger demand increases and domestic production decreases in reaction to the price reductions induced by the lowering of tariffs.

Correspondingly, the diversion of trade will be lower,

- the lower the external tariffs are with respect to country C;

- the lower the cost differences are between B and C (if B is the most efficient producer, there is no resulting trade diversion); and

- the more open an association is for new members whose accession may be motivated by wanting to avoid trade diversion.

In theory, trade diversion can be avoided completely if the third country's previous import volumes are kept constant by stipulating import quotas or by lowering external tariffs accordingly. In this case, a customs union supports welfare without putting the rest of world at a disadvantage (the Kemp-Wan theorem).

---

[18] In this context, there is also a recommendation to enter regional trade agreements with so-called 'natural' trading partners, meaning countries with which a large amount of trade is being conducted already. The idea is that they will tend to be efficient suppliers and therefore little trade diversion is to be expected. But this concept appears sensible only at first sight. In fact, it has been heavily criticised (for an overview, see Panagariya, 1999; World Bank, 2000, p. 41; Schiff & Winters, 2003, p. 66 et seq.). Among others, Panagariya points out that from country A's perspective, B might be a natural trading partner, but that does not have to be the case vice versa; further, A and B as well as B and C might be natural trading partners, but that does not necessarily apply to countries A and C.

In the case of a free trade area, the analysis becomes even more complicated (Panagariya, 2000; Zimmermann, 1999, p. 17 et seq.). Here, countries A and B levy different tariff rates *vis-à-vis* country C and rules of origin are agreed (e.g. provisions for minimum value creation within the customs union are stipulated). These are intended to keep imports with a lower tariff rate by B from C from simply being transported across the duty-free border from B to A, thereby circumventing A's higher tariff *vis-à-vis* C. In the end, the net welfare effects remain uncertain in this case. Individual examples can be identified in which free trade areas have more positive effects than customs unions (Zimmermann, 1999, p. 18). These are counterbalanced, however, by the fact that rules of origin increase transaction costs and may have a protectionist effect (see section 3.3).

Welfare effects with non-tariff barriers

In a world in which the tariffs of industrial countries are already rather low, non-tariff trade barriers become more and more important. Thus, the question arises as to whether regional trade agreements become more or less attractive from the perspective of an individual country. The analytical concept applied above to tariffs can also be applied to important non-tariff trade barriers. In this situation it turns out that the welfare effects are generally somewhat more favourable (Zimmermann, 1999, p. 33 et seq.).[19]

- With country-specific import quotas and an initial position as seen in Figure 3.2 (where country B is more expensive than C), trade is merely created and not diverted, because imports from C remain the same. If partner country B (with an increasing supply function) is the most favourable supplier at least for a proportion of imports, and if the import quota limited partner country B in its ability to export prior to regional integration, trade diversion can occur – which, however, is positive. Yet, import quotas no longer play a significant role in trade in industrial goods.

- When considering barriers to trade in services, which can be reduced in a discriminating fashion with regard to third countries (for example, rights of establishment), a similar concept applies as in the

---

[19] In addition, there is an area of literature – initiated by Krugman (1991) – that deals with the question of the effects on global welfare by the division of the world into a number of trade blocs. Nevertheless, such strongly simplifying assumptions are required that the results are barely relevant to decision-making (Winters, 1999).

context of tariffs concerning the possible creation and diversion of trade (and in this case also of investments). In addition, in certain cases liberalisation measures can lead to an increase in competition among domestic companies – thus raising competitive intensity not only through growing competition from abroad. The resulting additional welfare gain would be realised if, for instance, general market entry barriers were removed.

- If within the scope of a regional trade agreement measures are implemented that facilitate overall trade (for example, by simplifying customs procedures or by accelerating customs clearing in ports), this can in general be assumed to have a positive effect if it does not solely apply to the partner countries (as should be the norm).

Technical and other domestic regulations represent a trade barrier of particular importance. Where regulations differ among countries, transaction costs rise for exporting companies as they have to gather information about the regulatory requirements and may have to adapt their product and prove its conformity. These costs are real resource costs in comparison to the rents created by tariffs or quotas.

This difference renders a particular analytical focus on this issue worthwhile. Drawing further on Figure 3.2, country C is again assumed to be more efficient and can thus produce at lower costs than B. The regulatory requirements cause transaction costs amounting to t – which shifts S_B and S_C to S_{Bt}, S_{Ct}. As in the case of tariffs, initially country A produces the amount of 0-M_1 itself and imports from C the amount of M_1M_2 at price p_1. In this scenario, however, no customs revenue is incurred by the government in A.

If in a regional trade agreement between countries A and B the integration partner's product-market regulations are mutually accepted (country of origin principle), producers in B can offer their products unchanged and uncontrolled in A. Thus S_B becomes relevant again and the price is reduced to p_2. Country A hence produces the 0-M_3 itself and imports from B the amount of M_3M_4.

As in the case of tariffs, two effects can be distinguished:

- On the one hand, trade is created because a share of A's production is substituted with cheaper production from B (M_3M_1) and also, on account of the lower price, demand rises (M_2M_4). Consequently, total imports from A increase by $M_3M_1 + M_2M_4$. These effects increase A's welfare.

- On the other hand, trade is redirected in the amount of M_1M_2 because A is no longer importing this amount from C. Yet this trade diversion does not undermine A's welfare as in this scenario country B is not artificially cheaper than it was in the case of tariffs, but there is a real decrease in resource costs.

The effects on welfare can be graphically illustrated as follows:

- The consumers in country A benefit from lower prices and consume more (M_2M_4). Consumer surplus (and welfare) thereby increases by p_1EIp_2.

- This gain is counterbalanced by only one (not two) negative welfare effect: the profits of domestic producers in A fall by p_1DJp_2, because they sell less (by the amount represented by M_3M_1). With regulations, no customs revenue is lost.

- The net effect on welfare is JIED.

Thus, from A's point of view a regional trade agreement is much more attractive in the case of regulations compared with tariffs. In summary, this is related to a reduction of real resource costs that renders trade diversion from A's perspective not negative. Moving from the initial position to a regional trade agreement is thus clearly welfare-enhancing for A. The possibility of a welfare decline as in the case of tariffs does not exist.

Country A would benefit more from a multilateral approach, however, as C would be able to offer its products at lower costs than B. Moreover, it should be mentioned that the third country is placed at a disadvantage by diversion of demand.

This difference between regulations and tariffs can be significant as a brief 'back-of-the-envelope' calculation suggests. Based on a study on the bilateral trade agreement between the EU and South Africa (Lewis et al., 1999) the amount of lost tariff revenue is used as a proxy for the welfare difference between an agreement involving tariffs and a potential one involving domestic regulations. While the agreement seen from the perspective of the EU contributes less than 1/1000 of a percentage point to GDP – rendering a calculation of lost tariff revenue almost irrelevant, the effect for South Africa is calculated to be about 0.44% of GDP. A rough calculation for South Africa's lost tariff revenue results in roughly the same amount. Thus, in this case the welfare benefits from a bilateral agreement covering mutual recognition of regulations would be roughly twice as large as the effects of a mere tariff-related agreement.

Empirical results

As theory does not lead to unequivocal results about the welfare effects of regional trade agreements, the question arises as to whether empirical studies can help.[20] Primarily, one can distinguish two different approaches: On the one hand, trade effects of regional associations are considered. On the other hand, the focus lies on estimating welfare and growth effects.

When studying *trade effects*, the relevant data are usually examined in retrospect (*ex post*). Sometimes, general equilibrium models are used that approach this question from a theory-based *ex ante* angle. With *ex post* studies, an initial approach could be to observe the development of trade among the partners (or similar indicators) over time. Nevertheless, it is not necessarily the association that causes a possible increase of this indicator after the regional trade agreement has been implemented, because other factors also could play a role. In the end, the basic problem lies in the fact that one cannot observe how trade would have developed without the association.

The majority of studies attempt to overcome this problem with the help of so-called 'gravity' models of trade. These models are based on historic data and try to determine the most important factors that influence one country's trade with another (considering among other things the size and income of the countries, geographical or cultural proximity and transportation costs). If these factors are included, with the help of regression analyses one can examine whether establishing a regional trade agreement (as a so-called 'dummy' variable) has a statistically significant effect on the development of trade. This approach also has its weaknesses, however, because the question of whether one has really recorded all the relevant factors of influence always remains unanswered and these results must be interpreted with a certain degree of caution. Consequently, it is not unsurprising that different studies sometimes arrive at different conclusions concerning the magnitude of the calculated trade creation and diversion.

---

[20] For an overview of relevant literature, see Baldwin & Venables (1995), OECD (2001a), Soloaga & Winters (2001), Schiff & Winters (2003, ch. 2), Kaiser (2003, p. 97 et seq.), Lloyd & MacLaren (2003), Croce et al. (2004) and World Bank (2004, p. 57 et seq.).

All in all, no generally accepted conclusions can be drawn from the results that are available. As a rule, but by no means in all cases, a regional trade agreement contributes to creating internal trade. Further, concerning several associations, there are indications of appreciable trade diversion to the disadvantage of non-members, as is evident from the intensified European integration since the 1980s. The net effect of trade creation and trade diversion varies widely and can even be negative. Moreover, in the case of an association with a positive net effect is it not certain that the net effect is positive from the perspective of every country involved (World Bank, 2004, p. 62).

Effects on welfare can only be determined with general equilibrium models. These consist of a large number of mutually dependent equations that describe for instance the behaviour of enterprises and consumers, as well as illustrate the integration between domestic and foreign countries and between different sectors of the economy in a stylised form. Thereby, the functioning of a national economy should be roughly retraced and the effects of policy measures estimated as well. In reference to theory, three types of models can be generally distinguished – models involving perfect competition, models involving imperfect competition and increasing returns to scale and models that in addition map growth effects. Although this approach has its charms, it also has disadvantages. Some important elements in the model whose effects on the result can be significant must be determined more or less arbitrarily, because the required, empirically ascertained, precise data are missing. Hence, Baldwin & Venables (1995, p. 1633) call this approach "theory with numbers". Schiff & Winters (2003, p. 48 et seq.) also highlight the fact that deficiencies in the model can lead to an overestimation of welfare effects, for instance because the balance between trade creation and diversion is estimated as being too favourable (Lloyd & MacLaren, 2003). Therefore, again, the following results must be interpreted with caution, particularly as they represent only a very rough summary.

Increases in welfare can be shown for almost all members of regional trade agreements. Depending on the models used (types 1, 2 or 3), the increases are in the range of a fraction of 1% of GDP, of between 2 and 3% of GDP or of about 5% of GDP (World Bank, 2000, p. 50; Schiff & Winters, 2003, p. 48). As a rule, non-members are affected only to a small degree, but partially suffer losses of welfare as is to be expected. These losses are higher the greater the economic size of the association. Global welfare effects are hardly shown.

To summarise, it is important to note the following conclusion: as a general rule, increases in welfare are greatest in the case of multilateral liberalisation for the majority of countries examined.

3.3 Other welfare dimensions

Transaction costs as a barrier to trade

In comparison with the highly complex welfare effects, substantially clearer statements about the pros and cons of regionalism can be made if transaction costs are considered, brought about by the latest wave of bilateral and often overlapping agreements.

This tangle can be reminiscent of a 'spaghetti bowl' – a term coined by the economist Jagdish Bhagwati.[21] The problem lies in the fact that companies in countries that are a member of more than one regional agreement must observe different export regulations according to the country to which they are exporting. Consequently, the costs of information and of trade administration increase in comparison with an ideal situation of unilateral or multilateral liberalisation, in which the same (import) conditions apply to all foreign countries. Especially for smaller companies (as well as for those in developing countries) this situation is associated with relatively high costs and can have a trade-reducing effect. This is all the more important as with increasing trade in intermediate goods, today one product might cross borders not only once but several times at different stages of production.

With different regulations applying to different export countries, the key issue relates to the cost-increasing effects of preferential rules of origin.[22] These are needed in order to decide whether a good that is traded within a regional agreement by countries with different external tariff rates should enjoy the preferential treatment provided by the regional agreement or is classified as a third-country product.[23]

---

[21] The World Bank (2004, p. 39 et seq.) provides an illustration of the tangle of bilateral associations for different regions.

[22] See Krueger (1999), Panagariya (1999), Estevadeordal & Suominen (2003), Moïsé (2003, pp. 159-69) and Dieter (2004).

[23] Rules of origin are necessary in those associations that have no common external tariff (preference agreements, free trade zones or as yet uncompleted customs unions), since if every good that is traded between partner countries enjoyed

Rules of origin are often very complicated,[24] because in the course of globalisation production processes are increasingly divided and distributed across different countries. Hence, it becomes more difficult to decide where a good was produced and when it qualifies for preferential treatment. As a rule, a substantial transformation of the good must have taken place within the exporting member country of an association – although of course to determine this in an individual case can often be very challenging.

Another factor that raises costs relates to the fact that rules of origin can create additional trade-diverting effects in the case of a free trade area. This result should be explained in greater detail: if for instance it is required that a minimum share of value-added must be created or a certain production process must take place within the association, then more efficient suppliers of intermediate products and services from third countries can potentially be excluded. In this case, at the level of the intermediate product or service, trade is diverted (even if no external tariff is levied on the third country's preliminary product).[25] The more restrictive and more complicated the rules of origin become, the greater these effects are. Rules of origin can thus represent another gateway for a very subtle kind of protectionism. Therefore, these issues – which appear to be only technical details – are in practice often starting points for political interest groups to exert their influence. As a matter of fact, there are indications that preferential rules of origin are abused for protectionist purposes, primarily by the industrial countries (the US and the EU) in sectors that are

---

preferential treatment, it would be possible for third-country goods to be imported into the preferential trade zone via the country with the lowest external tariff rate, and then to a country with a tariff that is higher *vis-à-vis* the third country. In such a case this higher external tariff would be pointless, and the association would have the effect of a customs union on the basis of the lowest tariff (see section 3.2).

[24] Decision criteria in this context are a certain minimum share of value creation in the relevant country (for example, 50%), a prescribed production process, a transformation of the good that leads to a change in the classification of goods (for example, from fabric to clothing) or a combination of these. For example, for clothing to qualify for preferential treatment under NAFTA it must be made of yarn spun within NAFTA. Another complication consists of so-called 'cumulation rules', which regulate, among other things, whether input materials imported from third countries may be 'credited' in determining the preference of origin.

[25] Yet at the level of the end product, trade diversion decreases if more expensive input goods are used, and therefore the cost disadvantage compared with competitors in third countries increases.

considered to be vulnerable, for example in order to support the domestic textile industry at the supply level (Estevadeordal & Suominen, 2003). To the extent that this occurs, complexity of the rules of origin, and thereby also transaction costs, often increase further (as for example, with the NAFTA and clothing – see World Bank, 2004, p. 71).

Owing to preferential rules of origin, the transaction costs of trade can be estimated to rise in the mid-single-digit percentage range. On this point, however, only older studies from the 1980s are available (Estevadeordal & Suominen, 2003). These results are further aggravated if the rules of origin are not sufficiently transparent and potentially allow arbitrary decisions by the customs administration. The web of regional agreements and the international fragmentation of the production process further increase the cost-raising effect of rules of origin significantly.

In summary, the spaghetti bowl phenomenon as well as complex rules of origin hamper trade, and at the same time make the use of trade preferences appear less attractive. In fact, as the frequency of applying these preferences diminishes the more restrictive and complex the rules of origin become (Estevadeordal & Suominen, 2003).

Therefore, it would be of great practical importance for the WTO to harmonise the rules of origin, however; this ambitious project is unlikely to happen within the scope of the Doha Round. Even the politically and economically far less controversial issue of harmonising the non-preferential rules of origin (which is important for the definition of origin required for implementing anti-dumping measures) has come to a standstill.

A race for markets boosts bilateral agreements

As shown above, the global effects of regional trade agreements on welfare are unclear, and non-members to the agreements tend to be put at a disadvantage to a more or less strong degree. The rise in transaction costs as a result of a large number of overlapping associations makes matters worse. The continually growing number of bilateral associations at present therefore leads to some concern, even more so as the members of regional agreements do not sufficiently consider the negative effects on third parties or the higher costs associated with an increasingly dense network of associations. This situation basically implies a negative external effect, which, according to welfare theory, leads to excessive activity.

Game theory also predicts excessive and self-reinforcing regionalism. Because if regional trade agreements present advantages to an individual country, from its point of view it is the best (dominant) strategy to conclude these associations – regardless of what the trading partners do:

- If the trading partners pursue only the strategy of multilateralism, the individual country will receive better conditions of access to selected markets than the rest of the world.

- If, however, the trading partners pursue the more dynamic regional strategy in parallel with the slow multilateral progress, the country's own access to the markets of interest would deteriorate if it were to forego regional associations. Consequently, the country will try to re-establish a 'level playing field' with similar access conditions.

This insight especially applies to the large industrial countries, which – as experience shows – can exclude particularly vulnerable sectors from liberalisation when concluding regional agreements with developing and emerging countries.[26] Thus in the political process the resistance on the part of the import-substitution industry should be rather low and the interests of the export industry should tend to dominate, resulting in high levels of political pressure to conclude new regional agreements.

Because concluding bilateral trade agreements represents a dominant strategy for all countries, an unchecked race for markets can be triggered, as soon as some major players engage in this strategy and others feel forced to follow. In fact, this is exactly what seems to have happened with regard to the recent wave of regionalism. The race–for–markets view appears to be particularly relevant regarding the market interest of the EU, the US and partly Japan with respect to the larger Latin American countries (Mexico, Chile and MERCOSUR) and the emerging countries in the Asian region.

If the growth of regional trade agreements is getting out of hand and in turn really has negative global welfare effects, this race for markets would constitute the start of a self-reinforcing and increasingly detrimental process. In this case, relying on individual countries' incentives will lead to a damaging outcome from a global perspective. The best solution from a global perspective would be if all partners were to largely refrain from regional agreements. But this runs counter to individual incentives, and

---

[26] Certain trade sectors can be entirely excluded to a certain extent; liberalisation can be stretched over time or also be limited *de facto* by restrictive rules of origin. WTO rules do not prohibit this (see section 3.4).

there is the danger that certain countries could choose a free-rider option. Bringing the race for markets to a halt could thus be viewed as a global public good. This action would require the intervention of a supra-national institution endowed with the right to intervene. Yet such a body does not exist in the global context.

Coordination and arrangements among the involved trading partners with the objective of limiting this race for markets can provide a certain way out of this situation. For this strategy, the WTO offers the suitable framework. And within this framework, the large global trading partners – above all, the EU and the US – bear a particular responsibility.

3.4   Regionalism and the WTO

Regional trade agreements and WTO law

As the welfare-theoretical analysis has shown, regional trade agreements discriminate against third countries that are not part of the agreement, owing to the preferential treatment of the partners. On the other hand, the principle of the most-favoured nation (MFN) treatment is an elementary one of the WTO.[27] Accordingly, all foreign products of all trading partners should be treated equally at a country's border. This principle prevents trade distortion among countries. MFN treatment as a fundamental principle makes sure that from the perspective of an individual country, imports come from the most efficient supplier.

At the same time, at the multilateral level political realities must be accepted. Right from the start of the GATT, it was considered undesirable to renounce the instrument of free trade agreements. Accordingly, exceptions were created in the rules for regional associations.

Regional trade agreements lead to a reduction of trade barriers – and thus to a liberalisation of international trade – in line with a fundamental WTO intention. The WTO recognises this basically positive impact of regional associations and determines criteria that are supposed to limit trade-distorting effects. Art. XXIV of the GATT states:[28]

---

[27] For an overview of the core principles on which the world trading system is based, see Hauser & Schanz (1995).

[28] A similar provision is found in the GATS service agreement. Art. V requires that within the context of economic integration (for example, within the scope of a free trade agreement) liberalisation of trade in services may take place, provided that

5. Accordingly, the provisions of this Agreement shall not prevent, as between the territories of contracting parties, the formation of a customs union or of a free-trade area or the adoption of an interim agreement necessary for the formation of a customs union or of a free-trade area; [p]rovided that:

(a) with respect to a customs union, or an interim agreement leading to a formation of a customs union, the duties and other regulations of commerce imposed at the institution of any such union or interim agreement in respect of trade with contracting parties not parties to such union or agreement shall not on the whole be higher or more restrictive than the general incidence of the duties and regulations of commerce applicable in the constituent territories prior to the formation of such union or the adoption of such interim agreement, as the case may be;

7. (a) Any contracting party deciding to enter into a customs union or free-trade area, or an interim agreement leading to the formation of such a union or area, shall promptly notify the CONTRACTING PARTIES and shall make available to them such information regarding the proposed union or area as will enable them to make such reports and recommendations to contracting parties as they may deem appropriate.

8. For the purposes of this Agreement:

(a) A customs union shall be understood to mean the substitution of a single customs territory for two or more customs territories, so that

(i) duties and other restrictive regulations of commerce (except, where necessary, those permitted under Articles XI, XII, XIII, XIV, XV and XX) are eliminated with respect to substantially all the trade between the constituent territories of the union or at least with respect to substantially all the trade in products originating in such territories.

The conclusion of free trade agreements should proceed in a transparent manner. WTO members should already be informed at the time when such negotiations are initiated. Thereby, the WTO members that

---

liberalisation includes essential sectors (and trade volumes, number of sectors and supply procedures). This wording is much weaker than that contained in Art. XXIV of the GATT, which is likewise unspecified.

are not included are supposed to be given the opportunity to exert an influence on the creation of regional trade agreements. This consultation process is non-binding, however, and not used in general. The WTO's notification mechanism increases transparency, which can lead to reductions in transaction costs. Through the provision of timely information, manufacturers and traders can be spared unpleasant surprises and they are given opportunity to adapt to the new trade conditions.

The rule specifying that barriers to trade may not be raised with respect to third countries in the course of the creation of a regional trade agreement is more binding. Although this provision cannot avoid the trade-diverting effects of regional trade agreements, it can at least prevent them from becoming exacerbated by the construction of higher barriers to trade with respect to third countries. The rule is intended to prevent the establishment of 'trade fortresses'. The regulation expressly refers to the status of liberalisation in total ("general incidence of the duties and regulations of commerce"). This problem is especially relevant regarding the establishment and enlargement of customs unions. For political reasons, the partners of a customs union will not necessarily commit themselves to the partner countries' lower tariff rates. Thus the tariff rates of the EU were not negotiated, neither for example during establishment of the customs union between the EU and Turkey, nor during its eastern enlargement, but rather were taken over from the partner countries. In individual cases, this leads to increases in tariff rates with respect to third countries, which they are not obliged to accept without compensation. They can enter into negotiations with the partners and demand trade concessions (for example, general reductions in tariffs for certain products). If necessary, the WTO's dispute resolution mechanism can be used.

Also of great importance is also the GATT requirement that regional trade agreements must include "substantially all the trade" between the partners. This precaution serves to prevent sector- or product-specific 'cherry-picking' and is important to limit trade-diversion effects. Tailoring regional trade agreements specifically for certain products would open the floodgates to sector-specific associations that could put third countries at an extreme disadvantage. Assume that country A produces cars and no tropical fruit, country B grows tropical fruit, but produces no cars, and country C grows tropical fruit as well as produces cars. The temptation on the part of countries A and B is great to introduce between them free trade for cars and tropical fruit. Thereby, the automobile industry in country A and the tropical fruit industry in country B could selectively be promoted with respect to competition in country C. In principle, Art. XXIV bars such product-specific agreements. By requiring that the agreement cover almost the entire trade, targeted measures against competition from third countries can be largely avoided.

Admittedly, the GATT does not determine precisely what is meant by "substantially all the trade". Whether it is supposed to mean more than 99% of all trade or only more than 90% is subject to interpretation.[29] There is *de facto* the possibility to exclude 'sensitive' products and sectors (meaning in general agricultural products as well as textiles and clothing) from the trade agreements. This possibility facilitates negotiation because the resistance from the import-substitution industries will be less pronounced than in the case of a multilateral round in which predominantly developing countries are pushing for opening sensitive sectors in the industrial countries.

As a rule, trade among the partners of a regional trade agreement is not liberalised overnight, but on the basis of a liberalisation schedule. This way, tariffs are reduced quickly for unproblematic products but slowly for sensitive products. The WTO rules stipulate that a period of 10 years may be exceeded only in special circumstances. This rule is intended to make sure that cherry-picking does not have a chance to occur by way of disproportionately long liberalisation periods.

Trade among developing countries represents a significant exception. According to the Enabling Clause – a special clause for developing countries – such countries may grant each other trade preferences. In addition, this can be done specifically for certain products. The GATT requirement contained in Art. XXIV to include "substantially all the trade" does not apply to developing countries. Within the scope of the Global System of Trade Preferences among Developing Countries (GSTP), a number of developing countries make use of this possibility. Yet compared with the bilateral and regional trade agreements among developing countries, the system is fairly insignificant.[30]

---

[29] For instance, the EU assumes a 90% threshold (Lamy, 2002).

[30] GSTP member countries decided within the scope of the 11th United Nations Conference on Trade and Development (UNCTAD XI) in June 2004 to expand the range of products covered by trade preferences. Moreover, additional developing countries should be motivated to join.

The WTO rules concerning regional agreements are intended to minimise trade-diverting effects and in this respect are in principle very useful. They are not aimed at preventing regional associations, but rather specify criteria that should guide such trade agreements.

Unfortunately, regarding some important points, the WTO rules are too vague. Although in specific cases such points could be legally interpreted by WTO dispute settlement and enforced by retaliatory measures, this has not happened in any case of significance to date (Schiff & Winters, 2003, p. 255). In practice, with regional trade agreements proliferating globally, WTO members tacitly agree to tolerate such associations – employing the principle of not throwing stones at others when living in a glass house.

All in all, the WTO rules remain relatively blurred and complicate the WTO review process that is supposed to monitor regional trade agreements for compliance. The overall weakness of this mechanism and of rule enforcement can be traced back to the precedent of the Treaty of Rome (by the European Economic Community), which represented an offence against the rules for regional trade agreements and remained unpunished (Schiff & Winters, 2003, p. 249).

Regionalism and multilateralism – Building or stumbling blocks?

In order to analyse how regionalism and multilateral liberalisation are interconnected within the WTO framework, the discussion has so far focused on welfare effects. There are, however, other effects of regionalism – namely on the status and the development of multilateral liberalisation.[31] In this context, it is of particular interest whether regional trade agreements favour or impede the creation of worldwide free trade – the long-term WTO objective (Bhagwati, 1992). Regionalism may lead to incentives for raising or lowering trade barriers with respect to rest of the world. Above all, analysis should focus on whether the willingness for multilateral liberalisation is discouraged or promoted. In this section, arguments that the effects of regionalism are supportive of free trade are initially reviewed, which must nevertheless be put into perspective.

---

[31] For articles that provide an overview, see Krueger (1999), Panagariya (1999), Winters (1999), Zimmermann (1999, ch. C), Panagariya (2000), World Bank (2000, ch. 5), von Carlowitz (2003, p. 120 et seq. and p. 151 et seq.), WTO (2003b, p. 62 et seq.), Kaiser (2003, p. 187 et seq.) and Schiff & Winters (2003, p. 82 et seq., ch. 8).

Regional trade agreements serve to gather experience that is helpful for later multilateral liberalisation, for reasons that include:

- There is the potential that new issues of trade policy are initially tested in regional associations. The multilateral level might subsequently benefit from experiences with possibly different approaches and select the methods that have accordingly proven to be the best (see section 3.6). If, however, regional agreements create rules that prove unacceptable at the multilateral level and if these rules are not easily reversible, regional initiatives could be stumbling blocks.

- Especially in developing countries, governments can improve their negotiating skills and bureaucracies their competence for administering the obligations arising from the association. The administrative capacities can, however, turn out to be limited. This means that there is a danger that negotiations concerning additional regional agreements bind too many resources and therefore complicate multilateral liberalisations that are taking place in parallel. This could well be the case with the large numbers of bilateral agreements currently under negotiation. It is also possible that owing to a different range of issues at the regional and multilateral levels, the insights gained cannot be used within the WTO context.

- Consumers may recognise the advantages of cheaper imports and wider choice, and in future, as voters, may be more open-minded with respect to multilateral liberalisation.

Liberalisation with respect to the rest of the world could also be more readily enforceable politically if the import-substitution industry step by step becomes used to higher competitive pressure. So long as the rest of the world produces more efficiently than the partner country, and the partner country produces more economically than the domestic economy, regionalisation can represent a preliminary stage for multilateral liberalisation and bring about this familiarisation. To the extent that the import-substitution industry has already been shrinking in this manner, it may not be able to so effectively resist further liberalisation in future. Additionally, this sector will become more efficient, so that later adaptation to fiercer competition from the rest of the world will become easier. If, however, the representatives of the import-substitution industry recognise that multilateral liberalisation will follow regional liberalisation, they are likely to oppose the first step fiercely.

Likewise, this argument can be reversed in the case of an import-substitution industry that has strong protectionist tendencies. It is conceivable that the industry will grant its approval to a regional trade agreement only if at the same time it is assured that in the near future this will not lead to multilateral liberalisation, or even that – as compensation for increased competitive pressure – protection is increased with respect to non-members (for instance by means of anti-dumping-measures).

In theory it is conceivable under certain assumptions that the establishment of a regional trade agreement exerts such a strong pull on non-members that the end result is one single, large trade bloc – meaning free trade worldwide. Richard E. Baldwin has shown this in the context of his domino effect mentioned in section 3.1. Yet this line of thought does not take into consideration that existing members can refuse additional accessions. In fact, it is mainly the argument of market power that speaks for the fact that a trade bloc will not be global, but will end its expansion before this happens, because by increasing tariffs the own terms of trade can be improved at the expense of non-members. If the number of non-members continues to be reduced, this welfare effect is also diminished for the trade bloc. Looking at present-day reality, it would rather appear that a few large continent-centred trade blocs are likely to be established. Experience has also shown that membership applications are actually refused now and again, for instance by the NAFTA with regard to some Latin-American countries or for a long time by the EU with respect to Turkey.

This stage is where Lloyd (2002) sets in and demonstrates that bilateral associations can lead to crumbling opposition. In his studies, he assumes a trade bloc with several members, some of which refuse to grant accession to a third country. If an individual member country now concludes a bilateral agreement with the third country, the incentive for the others to likewise conclude a bilateral agreement with the third country increases, owing to the discrimination of the other members regarding market access to the third country. This incentive rises for the other countries in correlation with the number of member countries that enter into an association with the third country. In the end, it can happen that all the members eventually conclude bilateral agreements with the third country. From there on, it is only a small step to integrate the third country into the trade bloc. This process could even lead to the merger of different trade blocs and therefore represent a step on the path towards multilateral free trade. But it is uncertain how realistic this thinking is. To the extent that a member country with a dismissive attitude exports only a small amount to the third country, or expects, as it sees is the case with other member countries' existing agreements, that it must open up sensitive sectors, it will probably continue to refuse to enter into any agreement with the third country.

To the extent that developing and emerging countries use regional agreements to politically secure (lock-in) their basic intentions of trade liberalisation, it is evident that regionalism and multilateralism go hand in hand. For instance, Foroutan (1998) points out that in Latin America, countries have likewise lowered their external tariffs in regional trade agreements.

Progress in multilateral liberalisation is probably barely affected by bilateral agreements with respect to important facets of agricultural protectionism in the industrial countries. The reason is that although in the context of tariffs preferential treatment can be granted, this is not possible with subsidies for domestic production or for exports that are widespread in the agricultural sector. If subsidies are cut, all exporting trading partners benefit evenly. Consequently, the industrial countries and especially the EU will hardly become involved in giving up this 'internal' protectionism in bilateral agreements, because that would mean that a quid pro quo could only be offered by few countries, while at the multilateral level, the EU can count on much more comprehensive liberalisation concessions on the part of the developing and emerging countries.

A number of arguments support the concept that regionalism can have the effect of promoting negotiations within the WTO framework:

* For instance, it is occasionally pointed out that the establishment and the enlargements of the European Communities induced the US to push for dismantling tariffs in the context of the multilateral negotiation rounds of the 1960s and 1970s to decrease the trade diversion resulting from European integration (for references, see World Bank, 2000, p. 102). Conversely, it is said that it was the US that tried to exert negotiating pressure on the EU by establishing the NAFTA and the APEC during the Uruguay Round (1986 to 1993).[32]

---

[32] The World Bank (2000, p. 103) refers to an article by Fred Bergsten in which a high-ranking EU participant in the negotiations is quoted as having said that it had

This assertion is countered by the argument that other factors would have played a bigger role in the negotiations. Another reason often used to explain the lack of progress in the Uruguay Round negotiations is the restrictiveness of the EU's agricultural policy, which was presumably reinforced by the association's bigger negotiating power. In addition, the threat of regional trade activities runs the risk that the trading partner one wants to influence also adopts this strategy. In the end, it is very difficult to estimate the relevance of these influences in comparison with many other factors that have an effect on multilateral negotiations.

- The establishment of regional blocs can simplify multilateral negotiations because the number of the participants is reduced. Nevertheless, this argument is mainly of a theoretical nature, because only customs unions (can) have a common customs policy, and not, however, free trade areas that form the majority of the existing regional associations. In fact, it is mainly the EU that at the WTO level speaks with one voice. But this requires that prior consensus must be achieved among the EU countries. In the narrow EU context protectionist interests might succeed more easily than in the multilateral framework. In addition, a look at the WTO negotiations shows that different interest groups have formed (CAIRNS, G-20, G-90, etc.) which are independent of regional associations.

Along with the factors that tend to promote worldwide free trade, there are, of course, a number of arguments that support the hypothesis that regional trade agreements have an impeding effect. Multilateral liberalisation could then become more difficult to implement politically for the reasons below.[33]

- Interest in new markets by the export industry of any country could already be partially satisfied by a regional association, especially if important trading partners are already or are expected to become partners. Thus, the political pressure for more extensive multilateral

---

been the APEC meeting that eventually caused the EU to yield in the course of the Uruguay Round.

[33] There is a series of theoretical studies that pose the question of whether multilateral liberalisation is prevented by regional agreements. According to model assumptions this hypothesis can be either confirmed or rejected (for an overview of literature, see Winters, 1999; Panagariya, 2000; World Bank, 2004, p. 133 et seq.).

liberalisation might fall. It could well be argued that this is currently the case in the Doha negotiations, where – according to the European Commission – the protectionist agricultural interests within the EU are only partially countered by offensive liberalisation interests of the export-oriented industries.

- The export industry may even oppose multilateral liberalisation. Such opposition is to be expected where the export industry is in a position to quasi-artificially increase sales on the markets of the partner countries, because of trade-diverting effects and its preferential treatment when compared with competitors from non-member countries that are actually more efficient,. It will want to defend this status quo, which will be threatened by multilateral liberalisation. The greater the diversion of trade is, the stronger the opposition of the preferred industrial sectors will be. Because in the political process as a general rule it is above all the export industry that supports (multilateral) opening to trade, the dynamics of liberalisation would be severely curtailed.

- The same tendency applies in principle to poor developing countries to which preferential access to the markets of industrial countries has been granted. Their trade preferences are reduced by multilateral liberalisation as their advantages decrease with respect to the remaining trading partners (preference erosion). Hence, it is understandable that they view such a step sceptically. But because at the WTO level unanimity is required, progress in liberalisation will tend to be slowed down. Thus, the questions being asked are those of whether and how the individual, poor developing countries that are especially affected can be compensated for their disadvantages.[34] This has become a central topic in current negotiations in Geneva.

---

[34] The question arises, however, as to whether tariff preferences actually have any appreciable effect. In fact, studies show that the majority of developing countries with middle and low incomes will not be greatly affected by multilateral liberalisation, and that the more serious consequences affect a rather small number of countries (Alexandraki & Lankes, 2004). As a rule, trade preferences for developing countries work only if in addition to preferential market access other developing countries are simultaneously discouraged from entering the market by high tariffs or quotas. An example of this is the former EU regulation of the banana market, which secured a relatively high market share for bananas from ACP countries, but limited Latin American bananas by quota regulations. Also, one

• From the perspective of the industrial countries – above all, the EU and the US – which act as hubs in a hub-and-spoke system, bilateral agreements with a large number of developing countries and, above all, with the major emerging countries may be of more use than multilateral liberalisation (World Bank, 2004, p. 128 et seq.). A key reason for this is that the industrial countries must fear competition by other competing developing countries in the partner markets less than in the case of a multilateral agreement, in which the partners would lower their trade barriers with respect to all WTO members. Moreover, in bilateral agreements, the industrial countries can act from a position of power and enforce environmental and social standards for example (see section 3.5), something that they are not currently able to do at the multilateral level. Further, an incentive could consist of making slighter concessions at the multilateral level, so that the preference margins for bilateral associations remain attractive (Hilaire & Yang, 2004). Taken together, a certain danger exists that owing to these factors the major actors such as the EU and the US are less active at the WTO level and merely pay political 'lip service' to multilateralism. Nevertheless, in the Doha Round this does not seem to be the case, since both of these actors have contributed decisively to bringing the negotiations back on track after the setback in Cancun. Still, it is difficult to assess whether without their interests in bilateral agreements they would have displayed even more commitment, such that the Doha Round would have possibly made more progress.

Regional trade agreements can not only delay multilateral liberalisation, it is also conceivable that after establishing a regional trade agreement the trade barriers *vis-à-vis* non-members can even be raised. In developing countries this can occur without violation of WTO rules when the applied tariffs are lower than the upper limit agreed within the WTO framework (tariff binding). In industrial countries where this margin generally does not exist, anti-dumping measures represent an option for increasing the level of protection.

---

must consider that many of the poorest developing countries with largely free access to the markets of the industrial countries are able to exploit their sales opportunities only to a limited extent owing to a limited manufacturing base, lack of infrastructure, etc.

- This action can occur (as noted above) as compensation for the import-substitution industry in exchange for increased competitive pressure arising from the regional association. There are signs that in the course of stronger internal liberalisation the EU has intensified its anti-dumping stance *vis-à-vis* non-member states (Panagariya, 1999).

- In the case of a balance-of-payments crisis during which too much is imported and not enough exported, there is an incentive to increase tariffs in order to reduce imports. To the extent that stronger consideration is given to regional trading partners, the tariffs are increased merely with respect to non-members. This strategy can be seen, for instance, in the case of Mexico in the course of the peso currency crisis during the middle of the 1990s, when tariffs applied at more than 500 tariff lines were nearly doubled *vis-à-vis* many countries outside NAFTA; it also applies to MERCOSUR in the course of the Brazil crisis, when tariffs were only moderately increased *vis-à-vis* third countries.

- In developing countries in which the tax systems are often ineffective and custom revenues represent an important share of state revenue, reduced customs income as a result of the regional trade agreement may lead to an increase in tariffs with respect to the rest of the world.

- In theory, an increase in tariffs could also occur in customs unions in order to improve their own *terms of trade* with respect to third countries – domestic demand for their goods is reduced owing to higher tariffs and thereby the prices of the imported goods from third countries reduce in relation to export prices. The danger of countermeasures must be taken into consideration, however. Regarding the incentive to raise tariffs as a result of increased market power, theoretical models arrive at different outcomes (Winters, 1999; Panagariya, 2000).

In the end, no definite final conclusion can be drawn, either theoretically or empirically, as to whether regionalism represents an obstacle to global free trade. Although a number of arguments speak against this hypothesis, there are many indications that point in this direction. Once more, it depends on the individual case. The concluding summary below of the most important considerations underlines this.

- A bilateral or plurilateral association that from the start is motivated by protectionism (with strong diversion effects and possibly continually strong opposition by the import-substitution industry) will probably complicate global free trade. On the other hand, an agreement among countries that have as a basic principle decided to liberalise trade should not substantially impair the dynamics of multilateral liberalisation.

- Also, one must differentiate among the relatively few agreements that involve several members and the numerous bilateral associations.

  o European integration and the majority of other, earlier regional trade agreements with several members have up to now probably not led to a serious impediment of multilateral progress because, in the end, substantial liberalisation steps were achieved by previous world trade rounds, particularly the Uruguay Round.

  o When looking at bilateral agreements one must take into account that progress at the multilateral level depends decisively on reducing the 'internal' agricultural protectionism of the industrial countries and in particular that of the EU. Since in this key area, as explained, bilateral agreements barely serve as a substitute, they should not substantially impede multilateral progress. That being said, compelling arguments also support the hypothesis that multilateral liberalisation is being impeded, including:

    – To a great extent, bilateral associations in important countries may have already satisfied those export interests that are pushing for liberalisation, so that the political pressure for liberalising one's own market diminishes and the multilateral process is slowed down. Above all, this applies to agreements between industrial and developing or emerging countries, with which the large countries can for the most part achieve rather extensive concessions in bilateral negotiations and make more use of their economic power than at the multilateral level.

    – With the large volume of bilateral trade activities and the race for markets with which they are partially associated, it is to be feared that the attention of politicians (and administrative resources in developing and emerging countries) strays from the path of multilateralism.

–   Along with these concerns, it is evident within the scope of the Doha negotiations that a large number of poor developing countries that benefit strongly from preferential access to markets of the industrial countries view multilateral liberalisation very sceptically, and may possibly block it.

Reform of WTO rules for regional trade agreements

All in all, therefore, a certain degree of scepticism is justified, in particular with respect to the large number of bilateral associations. This view focuses attention on the question of to what extent the WTO is generally able to sufficiently channel the latest trend towards regionalism. As indicated at the start of this chapter, the key WTO rules that are intended to ensure discipline in the context of regional trade agreements are so vague that they can hardly be implemented in the course of the WTO review process.

In the current global trade round, the rules for regional trade agreements are a component of the negotiations agenda.[35] In particular, the issues concerning the individual wording of Art. XXIV of the GATT should be spelled out in a legally clear manner, especially what is precisely meant by "substantially all the trade". In order for this to have a chance of being implemented, the consequences of these rule specifications might possibly have to refer only to new associations and exclude existing agreements.

In addition, while a certain tightening of the rules is needed, it is only partly realistic.[36] For instance, economically it would be extremely desirable to replace the basic rule stating that barriers to trade may not be raised for third countries in the context of regional associations with a requirement to also lower barriers to trade with respect to third countries.[37] Yet, in the

---

[35] For an overview of individual aspects of the negotiations agenda, see World Bank (2004, p. 141 et seq.).

[36] For an overview of different demands for reform, see Schiff & Winters (2003, p. 251 et seq.).

[37] A central WTO concept is to guarantee to WTO members a balance of rights and obligations. It is assumed that the conclusion of multilateral agreements brings about this balance. If a member's rights are violated because another member has breached WTO rules, the balance is upset and must be restored (for example, by retaliatory measures). According to this concept, one would have to assume that because third countries suffer from rule breaches through trade-diverting effects

WTO system this would represent a true paradigm shift of the kind that can hardly be expected within the scope of the current negotiations. It would have to be recognised within the WTO that owing to trade-diverting effects, regional trade agreements tend to place third countries at a disadvantage and compensating measures are thus a general necessity.

3.5 The developing countries' perspective

Developing countries are in a specific position as regards the advantages and disadvantages of regionalism (Kennes, 2000, ch. 4 and ch. 6; Schiff & Winters, 2002; Schiff & Winters, 2003, p. 73 et seq.; World Bank, 2004). In this context, a distinction must be drawn between agreements among developing countries (South-South integration) and associations of industrial and developing countries (North-South integration).

South-South integration

With South-South regionalism, the static welfare effects can be more unfavourable than in the general case (see section 3.2), since the balance of trade creation and diversion should be more negative, especially in poorer and smaller developing countries. This result at least applies to similar goods, for example to agricultural products or to some simple industrial goods that are nearly identical at home and abroad and which play an important role in developing countries.

The object of consideration is a developing country A that concludes a regional agreement with another, relatively small, developing country B (Panagariya, 2000; Schiff & Winters, 2003, p. 35). Partner country B will not be able to produce enough in order to displace the relatively large third country C out of A's market. Then, however, the price of the good does not decrease in A, because third-country products are still being sold at the world market price plus customs. Owing to the lack of price reduction in A, trade is not created, because neither consumption nor imports increase. Instead, trade is only diverted to the detriment of the third country and in favour of the partner country. Integration country A loses customs revenue without profiting from trade creation, while partner country B benefits

---

stemming from regional trade agreements, they are therefore entitled to an improved market access. Under this interpretation, the upset balance would be restored by reducing the partners' MFN tariffs.

from higher sales prices in A and therefore from higher profits. Within the association in total, welfare decreases, as can be shown in a model. Because both countries mutually open their markets, and consequently the described effects are relevant in both countries depending on the product market in question, the disadvantages of trade diversion and customs losses are distributed over both countries. In this case, a country will be in a worse position if it has an appreciable balance of trade deficit with respect to its partner and/or if in the initial state it demanded much higher customs than its partner and thus loses more customs revenue.

In addition, the question arises as to how large the potential is for the creation of trade in the case of South-South agreements between two (or more) poor and small developing countries. It must be borne in mind that in such a constellation the differences in the comparative advantages may be rather small (when compared with the case of a North-South agreement). In these cases, trade creation in the intra-industrial segment is also low, because industrial structures are usually still not well developed. A certain potential for trade could arise if the countries are endowed with raw materials to different extents or specialise in different agricultural goods. A larger potential for trade – with which different comparative advantages also come into play – may arise when developing countries of different income levels conclude a trade agreement with each other.

With a view to the use of economies of scale, smaller developing countries can benefit from regional trade agreements to a relatively stronger degree because their domestic market is comparatively small, and considering the low levels of sales, the average costs of production are high. Additional export opportunities amount to an appreciable enlargement of the market. As a result of a (usually small) number of companies in individual markets, market expansion can also be expected to lead to a rather sharp increase in competitive intensity, which will make the companies more productive and more innovative. Both effects can serve to make companies in developing countries so competitive that they are able to compete in the world market. In this regard, regional South-South integration can be an instrument of development policy.

In these cases, however, there is also the danger of distortion of comparative advantages and of misled specialisation if relatively inefficient manufacturers in developing countries that are protected by the association's high barriers to trade benefit from trade diversion. In the past, there were indeed some instances in which a poorer developing country registered a strong increase in imports of overpriced capital goods such as machinery from its slightly more-developed partner country, resulting in considerable distribution effects to the disadvantage of the poorer developing country. In two cases it led in the end to the collapse of the association (in Kenya and Tanzania and in El Salvador and Honduras) (Schiff & Winters, 2002).

If with South-South integration these negative effects are to be reduced or avoided, an appreciable lowering of trade barriers is essential with respect to the rest of the world, because this results in trade creation, and diversion declines owing to the improved access of the third country. But the question arises as to whether unilateral or multilateral liberalisation is not fundamentally more sensible. Indeed, an evaluation conducted by the World Bank (2004) shows that more than two-thirds of tariff reductions in developing countries between 1983 and 2003 were related to unilateral steps and about one-quarter to multilateral liberalisation (Figure 3.3).

Figure 3.3 Developing countries – Share of tariff reductions between 1983 and 2003, unilaterally, multilaterally and regionally (in %)

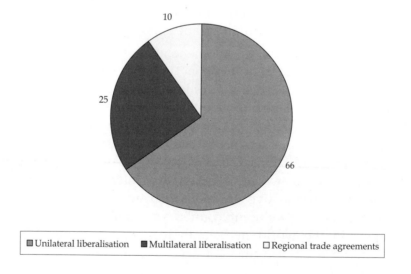

▣ Unilateral liberalisation　■ Multilateral liberalisation　▢ Regional trade agreements

Notes: For instance, 66% of the reduction in tariffs in developing countries in the period specified are the result of unilateral liberalisation. Figures do not add up to 100% because of rounding differences.

Source: World Bank (2004, p. 42).

Meanwhile, regional trade agreements (South-South and North-South) only contributed about a tenth. Certainly, another influential factor is that South-South agreements were not infrequently implemented either slowly or incompletely.

North-South integration

More positive welfare effects than in the case of South-South integration can be expected from North-South agreements, which at present more than 40 developing countries are making use of (World Bank, 2004, p. 30). Barriers to trade in developing countries are higher than in industrial countries, so that the danger of trade diversion is greater than in the case of North-North integration; thus a lowering of trade barriers is advisable here as well. Nevertheless, this is counterbalanced by a series of positive aspects, such as:

- From the perspective of the developing country, there is not necessarily a danger that the supply of the partner country avoids displacing a third country's production because of the larger size of the industrial country. Therefore, and as a result of the relatively high efficiency on the part of the industrial country's suppliers, price decreases and trade creation are more likely and should also be larger.[38]

- Further, the potential for trade creation is relatively substantial, because the differences in the comparative advantages between industrial countries and developing countries are generally rather sizable.

---

[38] Even if the third country's supply is not completely displaced, the prices of the products concerned will tend to decrease because the industrial country has a more differentiated supply of goods. Therefore, a price that is more or less uniform across the world does not result, but rather the industrial country's suppliers will have a margin of manoeuvre in setting their prices. If tariffs decrease for such goods, as a consequence their price would also tend to decrease in the developing country. Yet if the market power of the industrial country's supplier is very large, the company could also choose to retain or to barely decrease its prices and pocket the tariff reduction as profit. Intermediaries could exhibit the same behaviour in the industrial countries.

- To a greater extent than with a South-South association, the developing country benefits from economies of scale in production as well as from a higher competitive intensity on account of the considerable market expansion.

- Also, the growth-stimulating transfer of knowledge concerning traded intermediate and capital goods is more beneficial because of the industrial country's technological edge.

Further, developing countries can also look forward to an added range of advantages with North-South agreements (see section 3.1). They can secure access to a market that is important to them and more reliably solidify (lock-in) trade reforms, for example. But a number of conditions must be met:

- The rise in the developing countries' credibility depends on the likelihood of the trading partner imposing sanctions if the developing country fails to abide by the trade agreement. For instance, in the case of Mexico, the US has an interest in preventing the high levels of immigration that could be triggered by a cessation of reforms in Mexico with the expected negative economic consequences.

- Moreover, the question arises as to whether a multilateral reduction of trade barriers does not have the same effect.[39] The creation of multilateral investment and competition rules could also have an impact in the same direction.

- Other reforms, for example those combating inflation, deregulation, institutional reform or democratisation, are only secured if they are written down in the agreement or represent an implied condition for membership in the association. Although this occurs relatively rarely, it was relevant for instance with the Europe Agreements of the EU with the countries of Central and Eastern Europe, regarding democratisation within MERCOSUR as well as concerning the EU accessions of Greece, Portugal and Spain.

---

[39] Although regional trading partners are affected more strongly by a rescindment of trade concessions than the rest of the trading partners, and therefore the likelihood is higher that this behaviour will be punished, this is likewise possible within the WTO through its dispute settlement mechanism. Under the WTO mechanism, less-affected countries can join a lead plaintiff and thereby on account of their larger number would be expected to have greater potential for imposing penalties.

In addition, foreign direct investment from the industrial country (and the associated transfer of technology) can be expected in the case of a sufficiently stable economic policy, particularly if the developing country is to be used as an 'extended workbench' for outsourced labour-intensive stages of production. All these advantages can in principle also be achieved by multilateral liberalisation within the WTO framework; however, with suitable conditions, regional trade agreements may offer slightly greater advantages.

When compared with multilateral liberalisation, regional associations also have some disadvantages. Industrial countries certainly have an incomparably larger leverage in bilateral negotiations than at the multilateral level because of their larger market and are dependent only to a limited extent on the developing country's smaller market.

Hence it is not surprising if developing countries as a rule make larger trade concessions than the industrial countries (Freund, 2003) and the principle of reciprocity that applies to the multilateral level is consequently not applied here. Thus, the industrial countries as a rule lower their protective barriers for products from the developing countries only partially. Especially in areas such as agriculture as well as textiles and clothing, the trade barriers are substantially higher in the industrial countries than in other industry sectors. In regional agreements, these sensitive products are often excluded from liberalisation. Or, if they are included *de jure*, the rules of origin are often restrictive. If, for instance, a high degree of added value is required in the developing country as a condition for the country to be able to make use of preferential tariffs, this might possibly restrict its ability to export because the developing country – owing to its lower productivity and lower capital endowment – will produce with less value added than an industrial country.

By contrast with the multilateral level, particularly the US, but also the EU manages to secure labour and social standards in regional North-South agreements. At the WTO level, the developing countries are massively opposed to this because they fear such standards represent a gateway for new protectionism on the part of the industrial countries. If standards are prescribed that exceed the productivity level of the developing countries, their ability to compete would dwindle. In addition, where trade sanctions in the case of violation of these standards are possible, the threat exists that lobby interests will exploit this instrument in order to limit imports of competing products from developing countries more or less arbitrarily.

In the context of the NAFTA and some of the later bilateral free trade agreements, the US has pushed through rather extensive labour standards whose non-observance can partially be punished with sanctions (fines), which has not happened in the first years in spite of some complaints (Stern, 2003; Elliot & Freeman, 2003, p. 84 et seq.). In addition, the US has in bilateral agreements with Chile and Singapore implemented a ban on certain restrictions on the movement of capital, a breach of which is punishable by sanctions. This stipulation is cause for concern as capital controls can be important for preventing financial crises.

EU Association Agreements, for instance with Morocco in 2000, call for democratic principles and basic human rights, but are not supported by the possibility of sanctions (Stern, 2003) except for a complete discontinuation of trade cooperation in extreme cases, which is not very likely to happen. For a fairly long time the EU has been linking trade policy with environmental and socio-political objectives, as for example within the scope of the Generalised System of Preferences (GSP). Preferred countries can receive additional preferences upon request if they satisfy the EU's environmental and socio-political requirements. The partner countries, however, have only accepted this offer hesitantly. In view of this experience and the relatively low EU tariff rates, the effectiveness of these environmental and socio-political mechanisms must be strongly questioned. At the same time, these mechanisms contribute to making trade rules more complicated and engender legal uncertainty, meaning that transaction costs rise. In addition, further disadvantages must be mentioned:

- Regional, and in particular bilateral, trade agreements do not as a rule have effective dispute settlement procedures that are comparable to those of the WTO. Consequently, the developing countries are less protected against breaches of contracts on the part of the industrial countries.

- As far as a developing country is one of several among an industrial country's partners that have not concluded regional agreements with one another, investments may be diverted to the industrial country because only there does preferential access to all partners exist.

- Regional trade agreements do not offer as secure a basis as multilateral contracts do, because trade liberalisations can be more easily rescinded (although up to now this has rarely occurred). Moreover, withdrawing from the WTO is conceivable in extreme cases.

- In addition, it is a serious concern that with North-South regionalism, some smaller and poorer developing countries threaten to fall by the wayside, because industrial countries tend to select those countries that are of interest to them as sales markets or as extended workbenches. While the least-developed countries according to the UN classification enjoy free access to the EU market and in part also to other industrial countries, it is only those poor developing countries that are slightly better off that would stand to lose in a race for markets.[40]

- From the perspective of an individual developing or emerging country, the advantages of a North-South agreement diminish of course in line with the number of other countries that also conclude agreements with the industrial country in question. The World Bank (2004, p. 126 et seq.) has shown that for developing countries, negative welfare effects can be expected if all countries in this group conclude agreements with the large industrial countries. In the end, market access can be viewed as a positional good whose quality decreases as the number of users rises.

3.6 Is regionalism an opportunity for the 'new trade issues'?

Since the Second World War there has been an impressive reduction of tariffs. Although the worldwide average tariff level for industrial goods at that time stood at more than 40%, it is currently about 4 to 7%. In important industrial sectors in OECD countries, tariffs only exist in the amount of a

---

[40] Yet it must be borne in mind that many poorer countries in particular benefit from preference arrangements granted unilaterally by the EU and the US within the scope of the GSP, in addition to the EU's preference agreements with ACP countries and the preferential treatment given by the US to the Caribbean and ANDEAN countries. In the majority of cases, these arrangements exclude a large number of labour-intensive products for which the developing countries' export potential is particularly large (Schiff & Winters, 2002; World Bank, 2003a, p. 209 et seq.).

few percentage points. An entire elimination of tariffs is by no means utopian, even if in the current WTO round this objective will in all probability not be achieved. In view of this development, various 'non-tariff trade barriers' are increasingly in the spotlight.

Non-tariff trade barriers refer to all those barriers to market access that are not based on classical duties. They are very multifaceted and along with quantitative restrictions (import quotas) include for instance technical standards, anti-competitive practices, investment restrictions, the lack of protection of intellectual property and problems with customs handling. A large number of these non-tariff trade barriers make up the so-called 'new trade issues' for which (substantive) multilateral regulations must still be found. The issues are very diverse, so specific approaches are required. In this section, some of these important subject areas are discussed.

For quite a few of these barriers, the WTO already offers adequate basic rules; in the case of other barriers, these can be carved out in the near future. Yet there are also issues that cannot be appropriately addressed at the WTO for the time being, owing to the large WTO membership and the heterogeneity of the WTO's members. Do regional trade agreements represent opportunities to make progress with these issues?[41]

Government regulations often have different effects on domestic and foreign companies. Certain conditions can be relatively easy to tolerate for domestic companies, while for companies abroad they are associated with disproportionately high costs. Thus, for example, paying value added tax for companies established in the domestic market is a matter of course. For a company that offers its downloadable digital products worldwide through the Internet, this, however, is quite problematic. Even if national regulations are applied in a non-discriminatory fashion, they can have import-limiting effects. Government regulations are based on political processes and participation by the legislator. How can solutions be found in the legislative procedures that do not needlessly limit international trade? Here, regional cooperation can help, such as early cross-border information and consultation processes. Above all, it is important to make the legislator aware of the consequences of legislative activity on trade and to integrate the legislator into trade committees. Such cooperation with the legislature (and also the executive branch) of a partner country is most

---

[41] See also Pascal Lamy's (2002) overall very positive assessment of the chances of regional agreements concerning these issues.

easily achieved by bilateral cooperation. For this purpose, suitable mechanisms should increasingly be established within regional trade agreements. Unfortunately, up to now these are only developed to a small extent. For instance, the EU and Canada agreed to negotiate an agreement (the Trade and Investment Enhancement Agreement) that focuses on this type of collaboration in the regulatory area, but which, with respect to the EU moratorium on new regional agreements, does not include tariff reductions.

For many companies, it is primarily national *technical product standards and product regulations* that represent a big export obstacle. If they want to sell their product on the market in question, they must tailor it to meet the specific standards of this market or have its conformity verified. The WTO Agreement on Technical Barriers to Trade stipulates that technical standards and regulations should not be abused for obstructing imports. As a basic rule, the agreement prefers international standards to isolated regulations at the national level. But because exceptions exist, in practice a large number of national standards and technical regulations persist. Regional agreements normally do not include reciprocal recognition of technical standards and regulations. The EU domestic market, in which as a rule conformity in one country guarantees the simultaneous conformity in all other member countries, is in this respect a significant exception.

What could be arranged bilaterally is that the applicable standards of the contractual partner are considered as equivalent. This step would come close to the EU concept. It would also represent progress if certification procedures were recognised mutually. Such recognition means that companies could have conformity with the export country's standards or technical regulations certified in their own country (the mutual recognition agreements). The more countries give up national standards in favour of bilateral or plurilateral standards, or recognise equivalence, the less trade will be limited. Yet these solutions appear only second best, because international standards – meaning uniform regulations worldwide – should be preferred. In this respect, bilateral regulations can be regarded merely as a step in the right direction.[42]

---

[42] Nevertheless, it would be interesting to pursue the question of whether reciprocal recognition of technical standards and regulations might represent a sensible requirement for concluding regional trade agreements. Of course, national standards cannot be totally abolished, because specific national features (for

A lack of *protection of intellectual property* impedes the export of knowledge-intensive products protected by copyright. On the one hand, a company may be deterred from exporting its innovative products to markets if it fears that these will be copied without it being able to take legal action. On the other hand, the export of products worth protecting (e.g. clothes, movies and music) suffers in markets in which copied products are commonplace. Thus, the lack of protection of intellectual property can represent an important obstacle to international trade. In addition, it reduces the incentive to conduct research and development, thereby handicapping an important growth engine.

The multilateral agreement under the umbrella of the WTO concerning trade-related aspects of intellectual property (TRIPS) is a fully-fledged agreement for the protection of intellectual property. It regulates the scope and the duration of protection rights as well as questions of legal enforcement. The area of intellectual property rights can be seen as a satisfactory example of a multilaterally-regulated new trade issue, which renders bilateral regulations largely unnecessary. For example, the bilateral trade agreement between Vietnam (not yet a WTO member) and the US refers to compliance with the TRIPS agreement.

In many countries, sluggish, bureaucratic or arbitrary *customs procedures* inhibit the international exchange of goods. The more complicated and arbitrary the customs procedures are, the stronger the threat of corruption is. Regional cooperation can provide considerable relief in the area of customs handling. Thus, for example, the uniform EU customs code leads to a major simplification of customs handling for third-country imports as well. With customs unions, transit systems between the countries involved are unnecessary. In particular, customs unions can considerably accelerate and simplify the traffic of goods for third-country imports. Regional cooperation can further lead, for example, to the establishment of an electronic exchange of data among national customs administrations. Provided that access to these clearing systems is guaranteed to be transparent and non-discriminatory, third countries also benefit.

In spite of this, a multilateral approach that additionally leads to the worldwide modernisation and acceleration of customs handling should be

---

example, those concerning climate or security preferences) could demand internationally divergent regulations.

viewed favourably, as it again represents the optimum solution. Within the scope of the Doha Round, negotiations are underway for the creation of such an agreement. Of course it remains to be seen whether these negotiations will in the end be successful.

Through regional, plurilateral as well as multilateral approaches, trade facilitation has great potential to lead to considerable welfare gains. Although in this area a discriminatory application of facilitation procedures is conceivable, overall trade-diverting effects should play a comparatively minor role. Even determined followers of a critical view of liberalising international trade have little to criticise with trade facilitation, because it goes hand in hand with the fight against corruption and is an important instrument for enhancing export competitiveness. Practical solutions in regional trade can serve as a 'research laboratory' to identify examples of best practice and to derive rules for multilateral agreements (see for instance Moïsé, 2003, pp. 87-96).

There is a close interrelation between international trade and *competition policy*. Both have the objective of increasing the efficient use of resources, either by intensifying international competition through a reduction of trade barriers or by means of competition policy, for instance by taking action against a company's dominating position on the domestic market. Therefore, it is not surprising that at the time of creating the GATT, rules of competition were already provided for (Chapter V of the Havana Charter for the creation of an International Trade Organisation (ITO)). The project of creating the ITO was shelved, however, owing to resistance in the US Congress.[43]

Examples of competition problems relevant to trade include:

- By price dumping, a powerful company could ward off foreign competition on the domestic market.

- By exerting influence on marketing channels, such a company can also hinder competition from abroad.

- Several companies in one country can fix prices in export markets (an export cartel) in order to charge higher prices there.

---

[43] Approaches regarding competition policy are also found in the GATT Art. XVII concerning state trading companies and in the GATS Art. VIII (monopolies) (see, for example, Nottage, 2003).

From the point of view of economics, these practices should be countered by means of competition policy. Yet in many developing and emerging countries, the establishment of functioning competition regulations is only in its initial phases (Graham, 2000). Even if appropriate institutions exist, in many cases they do not have sufficient enforcement rights. This situation is unsatisfactory as a functioning competition policy is in every country's self-interest.

Currently, issues of competition policy are only rudimentarily regulated by the WTO (rules concerning measures against dumped imports and against trade-distorting subsidies and provisions in the GATS agreement concerning basic telecommunications and financial services). Of course, it would be desirable to create multilaterally binding, fundamental rules for trade-related issues of competition policy. But at present no consensus can be achieved in this regard among WTO members.

It is particularly important that competition rules are applied in a non-discriminatory manner, meaning that, for example, companies from third countries also have the opportunity to bring forward complaints against anti-competitive behaviour on the part of domestic companies. In addition, it would represent an important step to be able to punish the export cartels that are not forbidden in many countries. The fact that such export cartels are legal indicates that competition law in many countries limits itself merely to the effects in the domestic market, but ignores anti-competitive behaviour, which affects exports. This deficiency could gradually be overcome by bilateral cooperation, for example, in the shape of a trade agreement.

An important problem can arise in the case of mergers of large, internationally operating companies. Such mergers entail consequences for numerous countries, and in all affected countries, objections referring to anti-competitive law may be raised against the merger, as happened for instance in the case of the merger of the US companies General Electric and Honeywell, to which the European Commission objected. A multilateral regulation that provides for a worldwide notification system and for specifying a period for raising objections could serve to increase legal certainty for the companies (Davison & Johnson, 2002; Woolcock, 2003).

This brief introduction to the problem areas has already shown that depending on the type of question concerning the area of competition policy, it is partly a unilateral issue (e.g. regarding a ban of export cartels), a bilateral issue (e.g. concerning cooperation between anti-trust authorities) and partly an exclusively multilateral issue (e.g. with respect to a worldwide system of periods and registration requirements for merger control) (see for instance Petersmann, 1996; OECD, 2001b; Davison & Johnson, 2002).[44] If transaction costs are considered and the objective of creating legal certainty for the involved companies and market participants is taken into account, however, the multilateral approach as the optimum solution should be used wherever it appears feasible as an alternative to unilateral or bilateral solutions.

All across the world, a series of bilateral competition agreements regulates questions of cooperation among anti-trust authorities. Among these, the agreement between the US and the EU is certainly the most relevant. Admittedly, these agreements do not lead to substantially harmonised procedures. For instance, in individual cases they do not prevent national anti-trust authorities charged with assessing a given case from arriving at different results. The International Competition Network and the Global Competition Forum initiated by the OECD are approaches that are supposed to lead – on a voluntary basis – to an improved exchange of information between national anti-trust authorities and create the basis for improved cooperation. The UN's Set of Mutually Agreed Equitable Principles and Rules for Control of Restrictive Business Practises offers international guidelines for principles of competition policy. It would be important to bring together these various approaches for cooperation and regulation and to develop a coordinated system, for which the WTO provides a suitable framework.

In discussions, the demand for a WTO competition agreement is occasionally equated with the creation of a global anti-trust authority. These two approaches must nevertheless be distinguished from one another. The advocates of a WTO competition agreement generally support the development of binding fundamental rules of competition policy, but not the establishment of a WTO authority for assessing individual cases.

In the sphere of *cross-border investments*, multilateral rules exist only in certain areas. The service agreement GATS regulates the possibility to set up companies for the provision of services. Among other things, the WTO

---

[44] Numerous practitioners of competition policy see a solution involving international issues rather in a closer collaboration between national authorities. The International Competition Network created in 2001 represents such a platform with this objective (see http://www.internationalcompetitionnetwork.com).

agreement about trade-related investment measures (TRIMS) bans local content provisions that require that a certain share of the intermediate products must originate from the country concerned. Other items that are banned for instance are conditions that require a minimum export share of the total production. But there are no WTO regulations concerning the right of establishment for foreign industrial companies, the prevention of discrimination against foreign companies or questions of investment protection.

Particularly investment protection is to a great extent governed by a large number of special bilateral investment agreements. Naturally, the web of many bilateral agreements between investors of differing nationalities causes lack of transparency and *de jure* or *de facto* discrimination.

Uniform rules for all WTO members would solve this problem. But it is apparently politically not possible at the moment to negotiate a multilateral investment agreement. Hopes for negotiations in this area were disappointed during the WTO Ministerial Conference in Cancun. In this context, regional and particularly plurilateral agreements are nowadays the only way to strengthen investment protection and to further liberalisation of cross-border investments. Provided that liberalisation and protection are also granted to non-members in a non-discriminatory fashion, third countries do not suffer competitive disadvantages. That being said, the rights that are created by the agreements are up to now *de facto* limited to companies in the respective member countries.

International trade in services is in principle covered by the WTO. Since setting up the WTO, a multilateral service agreement (the GATS) is one of three pillars of the world trade system. The GATS system is based, however, on the principle of a positive list. Thus, every country defines the individual sectors that it wants to open to international competition (a bottom-up approach). An overall and sector-spanning obligation to liberalise, as is the case in the trade of industrial goods, does not exist. Therefore, up to now there has been only an initial, very modest step towards liberalisation. We are still a long way from comprehensively opening international trade in services, and the negotiations within the scope of the Doha Round are proceeding very sluggishly.

As a rule, bilateral agreements also liberalise some parts of trade in services. Of course, the concessions exceed the degree of liberalisation agreed in the GATS. They can tend to put service providers from third countries in a worse position. Hence, in this area, as with tariffs, discriminatory as well as trade-creating and -diverting effects may result. But there is no diversion of trade with a negative impact on the liberalising country if previously no foreign services were offered on the domestic market, which might occur in quite a few cases. Yet unlike tariffs, the WTO rules for regional trade agreements for trade in services do permit cherry-picking. There is agreement, specifically for each sector, as to which areas of trade in services are bilaterally opened. While in Art. V of the GATS there is a general requirement to liberalise as much as possible, a general requirement for opening markets as stipulated for the trade in goods (the requirement to integrate substantially all the trade) does not exist. Although the demand would be obvious to liberalise the entire trade in services in order to counteract the threat of trade diversion at the expense of third countries, it would hardly be enforceable politically, because service markets are regulated very strongly at the national level (for example, by proof of professional qualifications and laws governing the profession) and are partially associated with the physical movement of natural persons.

To summarise, it can be concluded that regional cooperation can make sense in the area of non-tariff barriers to trade. Nevertheless, it can also have trade-diverting effects. That is why attention should always be given to third countries having the opportunity to participate in the results of the cooperation in a manner that is as non-discriminatory as possible (through competition rules, for example,). Bilateral and plurilateral solutions represent an alternative especially in areas in which no consensus could be achieved within the WTO concerning the establishment of new sets of rules (governing rules of competition and investment). Further, such solutions can possibly serve to support WTO negotiations by developing blueprints for the new trade issues that can also be applied to the multilateral level.

4. Options for EU Trade Policy

Up to this point the study has highlighted the basic effects of regional and multilateral trade agreements. Now the angle shifts, and the trade policy options that the EU is facing are discussed from the EU's perspective. Indeed, the EU is an important actor on the trade policy stage; however, it cannot reverse fundamental trends. Therefore, the question arises as to how the EU will adapt to the present trade policy situation, in which manner it will be able to benefit and in which areas it should exert its leverage for the purposes of multilateral liberalisation.

4.1 Multilateral liberalisation

Comprehensive and far-reaching liberalisation within the scope of the WTO round initiated in Doha would be – as indicated in the foregoing theoretical analysis – the optimum route from the point of the EU. Only in this case is an essential reduction of EU agricultural protectionism conceivable, which would substantially contribute to welfare gains in the EU that are consistently higher than in partial approaches.[1]

Problems at the WTO level

More recently, however, since the WTO Ministerial Conference in Cancun the question of the WTO's political limits has emerged. In which areas is the organisation able to ensure liberalisation and what magnitude of liberalisation can be achieved in the short and medium term within the

---

[1] An exception is the scenario outlined by the World Bank (World Bank, 2004, p. 126 et seq.) in which the large industrial countries conclude bilateral agreements with all developing countries. Yet because many developing countries suffer welfare losses in this scenario, it does not represent a stable, long-term setup.

scope of the WTO? Is the organisation in fact suffering from its own success in the sense that WTO membership is continually growing?

It has become more difficult in the face of constantly rising WTO membership to achieve the required consensus (see section 3.4). In this context, some observers speak of the UN syndrome having possibly afflicted the WTO. Critics claim that breakthroughs in substance or institutional reforms can no longer be expected from the WTO.[2] Even the agreement achieved in summer 2004 on the framework for the negotiations does not constitute an exception. In view of these developments, some observers consider the WTO to be in an institutional crisis.

An added complication is that media interest in the WTO, especially during its ministerial conferences can entice some members to exploit the media for their political agendas. Ministerial conferences can be election campaign platforms, where governments can declare to have protected their country by vetoing the interests of the large industrial nations or from globalisation. This politicisation of the WTO carries a large inherent risk.

In principle, a solution to these institutional shortcomings could be to bring about a reform of the decision-making and consultation mechanisms. For instance, majority decisions could be conceivable. Yet such a reform would require unanimity. The also question arises as to whether majority decisions in view of today's understanding of the sovereignty of countries would be politically enforceable (see for instance Glania, 2004). For this to happen, a paradigm shift in international politics would be required.

Despite all these political problems, it should be kept in mind that the WTO legal system remains the backbone of global trade. Further, in the course of the regional agreements, difficult disputes are still settled by the WTO. Thus, for instance, to date the NAFTA does not prevent disputes between Canada, the US and Mexico from being carried out before the WTO; and, of course, these disputes are judged in accordance with multilateral rules. In the final analysis, however, the WTO legal system is also dependent on political intent, meaning the willingness to respect WTO rules and judgments. A WTO that is politically incapable of action exposes itself at least to the danger that doubts are nourished about its relevance. In the end, this could curtail the eagerness to implement WTO rules.

---

[2] With reference to club theory (Olson), one can argue that the WTO has grown beyond its optimum size. Some authors conclude that there is a necessity for a new, smaller, international organisation (Fratianni & Pattison, 2001).

Revised agenda of the Doha Round

In this context, it cause for concern that of the last three ministerial conferences, two have failed (Seattle and Cancun). The Doha conference in 2001 represents a creditable exception, although the success of the global trade round may in some way be attributed to the shock emanating from the 11 September terrorist attacks. Yet, the compromises that were found in Doha have turned out to be fragile, so that from today's view this conference was only a partial success. How feeble the compromises of Doha are has become most apparent with the 'Singapore issues' (investment, competition, transparency in government procurement and trade facilitation). While the EU originally assumed that in Doha a consensus had been achieved for entering into negotiations about these issues in Cancun 2003, some developing countries interpreted the wording differently – they insist that they have reserved for themselves the right to refuse negotiations. For the EU, there was virtually no other option than to postpone ambitions for new multilateral agreements on investment, competition questions and transparency in public procurement and the WTO round will no longer pursue these issues. Trade facilitation remains on the negotiations agenda, but it is not yet clear if an agreement can be achieved that is binding for all WTO members.

As attractive as the multilateral framework may seem in principle, it is not able – at least at the moment – to create multilateral rules in those areas in which it would be desirable (Table 4.1). Yet in the traditional area of tariff reduction, tight limits are also emerging. The high ambitions of industrial countries to substantially cut worldwide tariffs face scepticism or rejection by the developing and emerging countries. For example, in 2002 the US suggested abolishing all customs duties worldwide on industrial goods by 2015 (USTR, 2002). To date it is unclear, in view of opposition by some developing countries against a further opening of markets, whether a significant share of WTO members will engage at all in a reduction of tariffs. Some developing countries interpret the 'Development Round' concept as exempting them from having to make concessions, and merely the industrial countries should continue to open their markets. But this is what the least-developed countries fear since they currently enjoy duty-free access to the markets of the industrial countries owing to preference rules. The situation among WTO members appears to be highly complex. Even if negotiations only proceed in small steps, as they most likely will, the hope for concrete results from the Doha Round must not be given up completely.

Table 4.1 Global trade rounds to date

Year(s)	Place / name	Topics of negotiations	Achieved tariff reduction (in %)	Number of countries involved
1947	Geneva	Tariffs	19	23
1949	Annecy	Tariffs	2	13
1951	Torquay	Tariffs	3	38
1956	Geneva	Tariffs	2	26
1960-61	Geneva/Dillon Round	Tariffs	7	26
1964-67	Geneva/Kennedy Round	Tariffs and anti-dumping measures	35	62
1973-79	Geneva/Tokyo Round	Tariffs, non-tariff obstacles to trade, framework agreements	34	102
1986-94	Geneva/Uruguay Round	Tariffs, non-tariff obstacles to trade, rules, services, intellectual property rights, arbitration, textiles, agriculture, WTO establishment, etc.	40	123

Sources: Authors' compilation, based on WTO data (retrieved from http://www.wto.org/english/thewto_e/whatis_e/tif_e/fact4_e.htm) and Hauser & Schanz (1995, p. 42).

Such an outcome is conceivable given that by linking different areas of negotiation it is possible to achieve results that exceed the involved parties' smallest common denominator. The logic behind negotiating 'package deals' is that countries can obtain compromises beyond individual areas of negotiation. The possibility of discussing various topics in parallel means that countries may be prepared to make concessions that, considered in isolation, would be a disadvantage for them. It is important that from an individual WTO member's perspective the entire package represents an overall benefit. For example, such connections are made between negotiations dealing with agriculture on the one hand and services on the other. Some agricultural exporters have offered to carry out liberalisation in international trade in services in exchange for an opening of the European agricultural commodities market. Appreciable progress in these two areas in which the barriers to trade are still very high would represent a major success of the Doha Round.

In this context there are discussions about whether a round with a narrowly defined agenda might be more promising than a round with a broader scope. Fundamentally, finding consensus becomes more difficult if the possibility no longer exists to conclude compromises spanning several areas of negotiation. On the other hand, issues should not be placed on the negotiating agenda against which there is great political opposition among WTO members. The bogus compromise on the Singapore issues achieved in Doha and the resulting controversies considerably hampered the negotiations process for two and a half years. In view of this tense relation, it may be possible to derive an optimum scope for negotiations. The round should be large enough to allow package deals, but not be burdened needlessly by issues of negotiation in which consensus cannot be achieved. After largely abandoning the Singapore issues, the Doha Round appears to have approached a feasible scope of negotiations. As a result of this reduced negotiation agenda there is again a realistic chance of achieving progress and a conclusion of the round in the foreseeable future.

In view of the inner logic of package deals and of the only still remaining Singapore issue (trade facilitation) it must be borne in mind that one cannot negotiate this along the classical lines of concession and counter-concession. If a country modernises its customs handling, for example, that can hardly be considered to be a concession, since it also serves to improve its ability to export. Therefore, it would be absurd to demand concessions of other countries regarding the dismantling of tariffs in exchange for 'giving in' with respect to trade facilitation.

The EU perspective

In view of the difficult position the WTO is in, it is right for the EU to give priority to multilateral liberalisation as it says it would. This view is also heard from many other countries. Yet one must ask whether in part this only represents 'lip service', because emphasising the multilateral approach is certainly the politically correct view to take internationally. But in the political reality, doubts arise as to whether any real effort is being invested into progress on the multilateral front. The high level of activities as regards regional trade agreements indicate that many countries acknowledge that the WTO enjoys priority, but they are not willing to abstain – not even temporarily – from bilateral deals. For the EU, this political-economic rationale possibly plays less of a role, because classical foreign policy involving diplomacy still lies to a great extent in the hands of the member states, while the EU itself governs WTO-related matters. Thus it is not surprising that the EU gives top priority to the multilateral process.

The complex situation surrounding negotiations by no means implies that the EU must accept the state of the WTO as a given. It can contribute substantially to politically stimulating the Doha Round, in particular by being willing to offer a forceful and comprehensive liberalisation of the agricultural sector. The EU already took some steps in this direction, concerning the proposals to completely eliminate export subsidies, to substantially reduce trade-distorting domestic subsidies and to cut agricultural tariffs. It seems appropriate that the EU now waits particularly for emerging countries to table significant offers concerning a reduction of their relatively high industrial tariffs and concerning the more open service markets. But given this progress, in the following months more rigour in reducing agricultural protectionism will be required from the EU. In this context a French veto would effectively terminate the Doha Round and must thus be rigorously rejected by more liberal EU-members.

To sum up, from a theoretical approach, liberalisation through the WTO appears to be the superior solution. Substantial progress within the WTO framework leads to by far the largest welfare gains worldwide. In practice, however, multilateral negotiations are a tough, long-term project that can only be influenced by the EU within limits. Therefore, the EU must thoroughly analyse all trade options at its disposal and pursue a differentiated strategy.

4.2   Unilateral reduction of tariffs

In discussions on trade policy, quite often the importance of unilateral tariff reductions is underestimated considerably. Figure 3.3 in the previous chapter shows that in the period 1983-2003, the unilateral (autonomous) dismantling of tariffs by developing countries represented 66% of all tariff reductions, while multilateral liberalisation represented 25% and regional agreements a mere 10%.

According to international trade theory, tariffs have several effects (see chapter 3, section 3.2). They increase domestic prices and displace domestic consumption, which is detrimental to welfare. On the other hand, they possess three useful effects. They serve to earn income for the country, gainfully protect the domestic economy against foreign competition, and in certain circumstances permit the development of promising industrial sectors in the context of a strategic trade policy. If one takes the example of the EU, however, the question arises as to whether tariffs can or should in general still fulfil these functions today.[3]

About 130,000 customs officers of the EU-15 realise customs revenue of about €11 billion. Thus, each customs officer statistically generates €85,000 in customs revenue. According to the EU, the weighted average of the applied non-agricultural tariffs to which third-country imports are subject amounts to about 1.6%. If expenses for staff, material and other items of customs administration are added, the costs involved will be found to exceed income.[4]

In many industries, tariff rates are at levels that no longer possess any recognisable protective function. Those products for which extensive efforts at marketing and after-sales service are pursued and products whose production costs in third countries are considerably below the EU level are not noticeably protected from foreign competition by tariff rates of between 3 and 5%. Many products of industrial countries are aimed at the high quality end of the market and consumers (or industrial end users) are prepared to pay a higher price for them. Hence, small price differences do not have any real significance, particularly in the case of branded products. Consequently, low tariff rates do not play an appreciable role on these markets. In addition, exchange rates are able to vary widely within a rather short period, even in a double-digit range, thus exerting much greater influence on the international price structure.

Admittedly, there are also areas in which even low tariffs can have a relatively strong protective effect. With commodities[5] (e.g. crude oil, metals

---

[3] Regarding arguments in favour of an elimination of industrial tariffs see also Slaughter (2003).

[4] In this context, it must of course be borne in mind that the task of the customs officers transcends the generation of revenue, and includes for instance the fight against brand piracy and preventing the import of prohibited objects (for example by the Convention on International Trade in Endangered Species of Wild Flora and Fauna).

[5] Commodities are characterised by the fact that they exhibit no unique characteristic, meaning they are interchangeable. The manufacturing country is unimportant and stock exchange dealings are possible.

and agricultural products) and industries that exhibit a large input of raw materials there is a high degree of transparency regarding prices and price competition; and even small cost differences (as with tariffs, in the range of a few percentage points) can decisively influence the ability to compete. The same applies if the proportion of value added for any domestically manufactured product is very low (high effective protection).

The argument of strategic trade policy has been controversial for a long time. It concerns the question of whether tariffs (or subsidies) can serve to initially provide benefits to infant industries or to increase domestic companies' profits at the expense of those firms situated abroad (Matthes, 2004, p. 25). The key issue in this criticism are strong doubts about whether governments are able to recognise the promising industrial sectors. The problematic aspect is that they can be influenced in their choice by interest groups that have strong incentives to show that their industry is suitable. Strategic trade policy can also provoke counter-reactions on the part of the trading partner, which can even lead to trade wars.

That being said, consideration must be given to whether the EU would not do itself a favour by abolishing tariffs completely – or at least in many sectors. This step would facilitate the reduction of companies' and consumers' cost burdens, without causing markedly increased adjustment costs for companies competing with imports. Reduced budgetary income would be compensated by reductions in the cost of customs administration.

A unilateral reduction of tariffs would nevertheless be problematic in the negotiating process, because international negotiations about a further reduction of tariffs follow a mercantilist blueprint. According to this concept, the dismantling of one's own trade barriers is seen as a concession. By unilaterally reducing tariffs, the EU would therefore be seen to be needlessly spending its bargaining chips.

In this context it must be borne in mind that – as mentioned earlier – a reduction of tariffs is also achievable outside WTO tariff negotiations. For developing and emerging countries it is not a matter of abolishing the remaining tariffs because of administrative expenses, but rather of promoting their integration into the global economy by lowering their tariff rates to a tolerable level. Here it is also being realised that excessive tariff rates harm a country's own economy. The reduction of almost prohibitively high tariffs can often lead to increased tariff revenues through higher imports and reduced corruption. The trend towards unilaterally reducing tariffs is by no means unreal, but rather corresponds to political realities, as evident not only from statistics, but for instance by recent developments in India. There, in the course of economic reform, peak tariffs and the overall tariff levels saw repeated and significant reductions.

4.3   Bilateral agreements

In chapter 3, section 3.2, the welfare effects of regional (and bilateral) trade agreements are shown to be theoretically ambivalent from an individual country's perspective. Empirically, positive welfare effects of various degrees are the rule. Focusing on the EU, empirical studies of different bilateral agreements such as those with Turkey (De Santis, 1998), South Africa (Lewis et al., 1999) and Mexico (Slootmaekers, 2004) find almost no trade-diverting effects of these agreements, so the welfare impact is revealed (or if not explicitly calculated in the respective study it can be assumed) to be positive. Yet, as trade volumes with these countries are small in relation to total EU trade, the welfare contribution is only minimal.

Nevertheless, the EU has a certain incentive to conclude bilateral agreements on tariffs. As also discussed in section 3.2, the welfare-driven incentive would be even greater if non-tariff trade barriers were to be put on the agenda. An important case in point is found in domestic regulations, where trade diversion would not occur, but instead a reduction in real resource costs would take place. Moreover, negotiations about trade liberalisation with regard to domestic regulation are very complex. Thus, the advantage of lower transaction costs in bilateral agreements is all the more significant with this topic.

The incentives for bilateral agreements are even larger when trade-diverting effects are to be expected owing to the trade agreements of other countries (such as that of the US with Mexico) and to the political pressure exerted by the exporting industry to conclude bilateral agreements to re-establish a level playing field.

A political-economy argument also discards the case for a multilateral agreement to a certain degree. The largest welfare gains for the EU would result from a lowering (or elimination) of tariffs and subsidies in agriculture. Realistically, a cut in subsidies can only be expected in a multilateral framework, as all countries exporting to the EU would benefit from such a step (see chapter 3, section 3.4). Thus, the EU will not be prepared to cut subsidies in a bilateral or regional trade agreement since it will not be able to obtain as large a quid pro quo as in a multilateral context. This could represent a very strong argument for giving priority to the WTO. Yet in the mercantilist approach with which multilateral trade negotiations are conducted, the positive welfare contribution of lowering one's own protectionism does not count much. What counts more are the trade liberalisation measures of other countries that can be expected from the Doha Round. These, however, might not be very relevant with regard to emerging countries, which are the particular focus of the EU's interest. As tariff reduction formulas refer to bound tariff rates and as many emerging countries' bound tariffs far exceed applied tariffs, the *de facto* liberalisation agreed upon in the Doha Round might not be substantial. Thus the negotiating value of agricultural subsidies might not be worth as much as suggested in the multilateral context.

Overall, the EU has relatively strong incentives to conclude bilateral agreements, especially with regard to non-tariff barriers such as domestic regulation issues, where the welfare effects are clearly positive and the WTO process lags far behind.

In this respect, the EU perspective therefore does not necessarily correspond to the perspective of global economic welfare. As the analysis in chapters 2 and 3 revealed, the trend towards bilateral agreements currently seems to be gaining ground and, in part, bears the hallmarks of a race for markets. The transaction costs of global trade increase as a result of the large number of overlapping agreements (the 'spaghetti bowl phenomenon') along with the associated and sometimes very complicated rules of origin, thereby particularly affecting smaller companies and those in developing countries. The resulting global welfare effects need not be positive. Nevertheless, the EU must accept this trend towards bilateralism to a certain degree as a given.

Thus, from the selfish EU perspective, the question is with which trading partners bilateral trade agreements are most promising (see Table 4.2). In this context, the US first comes to mind, which in 2003 received more than one-quarter of the EU's exports outside the EU. Yet a tacit agreement exists between leading OECD countries to abstain from regional trade agreements among industrial countries in different regions of the world.

Table 4.2 The markets of the EU-25 countries

	Share of extra EU-25 exports in 2003 (in %)	Change in the share between 1999 and 2003, (in %)
Europe without the EU-25, incl.	**24.8**	**2.3**
Switzerland	8.1	-1.2
Norway	3.1	-0.3
Turkey	3.3	0.3
Bulgaria, Romania	2.3	0.8
America, incl.	**34.0**	**-3.2**
NAFTA	29.7	-1.3
the US	25.7	-1.4
Canada	2.4	0.0
Latin America	5.0	-1.7
Asia, incl.	**29.4**	**1.3**
Japan	4.6	-0.5
China	4.7	1.8
ASEAN	4.4	-0.2
Dynamic Asian Economies (DAE)	8.5	-0.7
Commonwealth of Independent States, incl. the	6.0	2.4
Russian Federation	4.2	1.8
Oceania	**2.5**	**0.0**
Africa	**8.0**	**-0.4**
Not recorded	1.3	0.0
For information only		
ACP countries	**4.8**	**0.0**
Mediterranean area	**11.4**	**-0.3**

Notes: NAFTA – the US, Canada, Mexico

ASEAN – Brunei, Indonesia, Cambodia, Laos, Myanmar, Malaysia, the Philippines, Singapore, Thailand, Vietnam

DAE – Hong Kong, Malaysia, Singapore, South Korea, Taiwan, Thailand

Oceania – including Australia, New Zealand, polar areas

Source: Eurostat, New Cronos database and authors' calculations.

Transatlantic free trade zone

Admittedly, over the course of many years there have been repeated attempts by business and certain political factions to create a transatlantic free trade zone.[6] So far, governments have unequivocally rejected such attempts. Instead, various cooperation forums are used to reduce non-tariff trade barriers (for example, the Transatlantic Business Dialogue).

On average, the tariff rates in transatlantic trade are relatively low. Transatlantic trade is impaired much more strongly by a large number of non-tariff barriers. These barriers mostly concern questions of collaboration by authorities and legislatures. Issues of negotiations include, for instance, mutual recognition of standards and certifications, high bureaucratic expenses in the context of delegating staff, problems in customs handling (for example, different application of EU customs regulations depending on the country involved) and divergent legal standards. Various business fora have repeatedly pointed out the specific obstacles over recent years. The politically responsible bodies were called upon to initiate steps for overcoming these trade barriers. Because as a rule this would require the consultation and active participation of parliaments and authorities, the results of these efforts have been rather modest.

While until now a transatlantic free trade agreement was considered taboo, agreements within the world's geographical regions (for example, by the US and Canada or the EU itself) were on the other hand seen as legitimate. The reason for the strong restraint exercised by the industrial countries in creating region-spanning associations among themselves is the view that these would have significant trade-creating and -diverting effects among certain important industrial countries, putting third countries at a considerable disadvantage. If the EU and the US regulated their trade bilaterally, so the argument goes, the relevance of the multilateral trade order would diminish considerably. Therefore, with respect to the multilateral system, non-tariff trade barriers should be removed by, for example, the reciprocal recognition of certification procedures (mutual recognition agreements), but by no means by tariffs. Thus, the industrial countries have taken consideration of less-developed countries at their own expense.

---

[6] For details concerning the relevant academic literature, Langhammer et al. (2002) presents a short overview of the activities within the scope of the annual EU-US summits since 1995 as well as a current analysis of the topic.

The paradigm according to which the 'elephants' of world trade should refrain from concluding comprehensive bilateral agreements with each other that include tariffs can be questioned using various arguments:

- The WTO legal system would not necessarily be called into question by bilateral agreements. Often, in bilateral agreements, arbitration is rather non-binding and regulated in more traditional diplomatic, consultative ways. Independent dispute settlement with judicial functions is usually not provided for. As a result, in the case of bilateral agreements there are often no retorsion measures with which to efficiently sanction rule violations. Thus, despite the NAFTA, Canada and the US often still carry out their trade disputes through the WTO. The EU may serve as a counter-example because it regulates trade disputes among its members internally. The EU legal system (with the European Court of Justice), however, represents a unique case worldwide that became possible only on the back of deep integration and the transfer of sovereignty to a supranational level.

- To a large extent trade among industrial countries consists of similar products. Between the EU and the US, the reciprocal exchange of goods concentrates on higher-value industrial products (see Figure 4.1). Cars coming from the EU are sold in the US and vice versa. Accordingly, trade hardly takes place on the basis of comparative cost advantages. Rather, companies use rising returns to scale and the chance to serve several markets from one production base. In addition, consumers appreciate a wide choice and international trade expands the range of options from which they can choose. The reason for strong trade among industrial countries is often the progressive, company-driven integration of the markets. International economic relations are characterised by a close integration of foreign direct investment and intra-company trade. Multinational companies invest internationally and trade takes place in different countries among the companies belonging to the same group. This situation particularly applies to the EU and the US. About 57% of EU exports to the US in 2002 consisted of trade among affiliated companies. For Germany, this proportion was even higher, at about 67% (Hamilton & Quinlan, 2004).

*Figure 4.1 Structure of transatlantic trade according to product categories –
Share of EU-25 extra trade with the US (in %)*

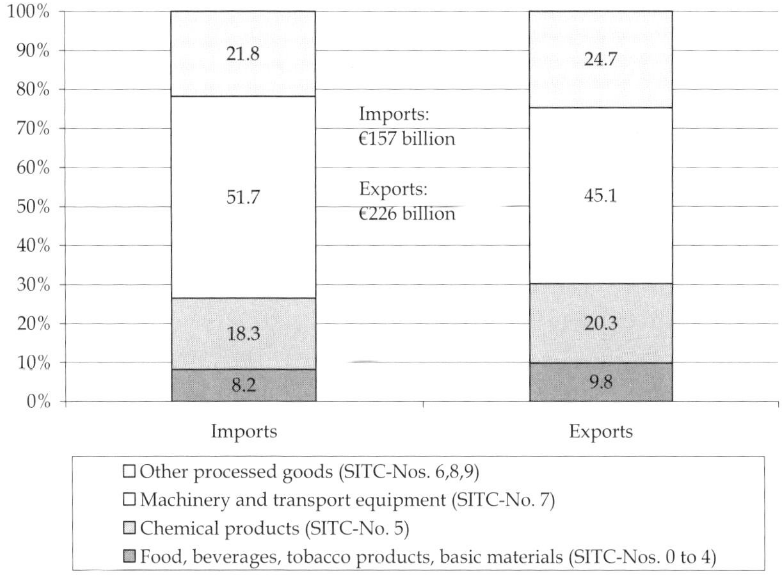

Note: Status as of 2003.

Sources: Eurostat (New Cronos Database) and authors' calculations.

The transatlantic dismantling of tariffs for industrial goods is less problematic in this context,[7] because bilateral agreements concerning tariffs do not essentially change these determinants for trade among industrial countries. This argument applies, above all, to the intensive integration of multinational companies. In addition, modern manufactured products, for which marketing and after-sales service play an important role for instance, are hardly protected by low tariffs (see section 4.2).

Nevertheless, trade-diverting effects on third industrial countries cannot be completely ruled out, although here the argument also applies that tariff rates are relatively low. On the other hand, similar

---

[7] The rationale stated here does not apply to agricultural products, for which trade barriers in the EU and the US are still substantially higher. Therefore, it must be reckoned that the agricultural sector will continue to be largely excluded from a transatlantic agreement.

products (for example, cars and machinery) are traded among industrial countries for which a country's respective competitive advantage is substantially lower than for instance in the trade of different products with developing countries (for example, clothing and machinery). Accordingly, a free trade agreement between the US and the EU could primarily affect other OECD countries, such as Japan. Any such impact would be enhanced if important areas relevant to trade that go beyond tariffs and in which the trade barriers are still more prominent are liberalised. These resulting discriminations could be counteracted in different ways: by the opportunity for other countries to join the association (on open regionalism, see Langhammer et al., 2002), by parallel conclusion of different agreements or preferably by the conclusion of one agreement that from the start includes the leading exporting nations (see section 4.4).

- At the same time, with respect to the poorer developing countries, no major distortion of trade should result from an abolition of tariffs between the EU and the US.[8] Thus, for instance, neither the American nor the European clothing industries will considerably increase their ability to compete in the case of a bilateral agreement between the EU and the US in comparison with their Chinese competitors, because the Chinese cost advantages are significantly greater than the level of tariffs on most clothing products. During recent years, exchange rate fluctuations have led to much stronger cost movements than would have resulted from the abolition of tariffs, without having had any serious impact on the basic structure of trade. In other words, the markets are relatively strongly segmented between the products of industrial countries and imports from developing countries, so that the discontinuation of customs-related cost burdens in the amount of a few percentage points should have no significant consequences on the direction of the trade flow. A key trigger for trade between

---

[8] Of course, there are individual, mostly labour-intensive, manufactured products for which the EU and the US still levy tariffs in the lower double-digit range. The US for instance currently charges a tariff rate of more than 30% on certain woollen fabrics, glass and ceramic products. Here trade diversion at the expense of developing countries cannot be excluded. Yet tariffs on the prevailing majority of manufactured products are so low that they offer no appreciable protection from competition from much more competitive developing and emerging countries.

industrial and developing countries – the different endowments of production factors – would remain unaffected by regional trade agreements among industrial countries. To the extent that (albeit limited) trade-distorting effects may appear with respect to developing and emerging countries, these could be reduced by the growth benefits stemming from the discussed agreement and by the associated rise in incomes and higher demand for imports by partners. Also, when concluding such an association, one could at the same time autonomously reduce tariff rates *vis-à-vis* third countries.

On more careful inspection, the paradigm according to which a transatlantic free trade zone that includes tariffs would cause great economic harm to global trade must be revisited. Anyhow, such a step is not necessarily advisable for other reasons.

Macroeconomically, one should not expect too much from such a free trade zone, because bilateral trade is already quite strongly liberalised owing to the low levels of tariffs (Langhammer et al., 2002). Also, with regard to non-tariff barriers to trade, the problems from an overall economic point of view lie rather in the area of 'fine tuning'. By contrast, multilateral liberalisation is far more significant. Thus, for example, Baldwin & Francois (1996) conclude that with the creation of a transatlantic economic area, GDP in the EU as well as in the NAFTA could be expected to grow by about $20 billion each (at 1992 US prices), while a worldwide liberalisation would mean that approximately $220 billion would be attainable for the EU-15 and about $90 billion for the NAFTA. In addition, a plurilateral approach of similar scope would also be conceivable within the OECD framework, which would likewise lead to much higher gains in welfare than an association between the EU and the US (see section 4.4).

Further, a transatlantic free trade agreement must not only be assessed economically, but also politically. The EU and the US represent the political pillars of the multilateral system. In spite of the relatively modest effects in economic terms, by establishing a bilateral free trade agreement they would be sending out a political signal that would probably tend to weaken the WTO.

Transatlantic trade and investment agreements

Therefore, an approach that takes into account the special transatlantic economic relationship as well as the overall political responsibility of both elephants is obvious. This approach consists of two elements:

- A bilateral trade and investment agreement that excludes tariffs in consideration of multilateral tariff reductions would represent one element that could facilitate movement towards the objective of a transatlantic economic area. Such an agreement (sometimes called a partnership or friendship treaty)[9] would in particular address the special issues of the bilateral trade in services and technical regulation as well as those of investment and competition. It would follow the approach used for the Trade and Investment Enhancement Agreement that is to be negotiated between the EU and Canada. Such an agreement would provide a legal framework to improve the collaboration between authorities and legislatures, and to stipulate appropriate provisions for transatlantic economic relations. With respect to third countries, discriminating effects from this kind of regulatory fine-tuning could not be ruled out completely; however, these would remain limited.[10] Admittedly, such an agreement would face the challenge of going beyond the declarations of good intentions and of really finding regulations and mechanisms that remove the existing obstacles. Hence, it remains to be seen whether these high expectations can actually be fulfilled.

- In the area of tariffs, in consideration of the joint political responsibility for the multilateral system one would continue to bank on solutions under the umbrella of the WTO (concerning the general

---

[9] This idea has already been introduced in the discussions concerning the creation of the transatlantic marketplace. For instance, the umbrella organisation of the European federations of industries and employers' associations, UNICE (*Union des Industries de la Communauté Européenne*), is demanding such a transatlantic 'friendship agreement'.

[10] Trade-diverting effects are not to be expected if the temporary delegation of employees by multinational companies from the EU to the US, which is currently often arranged rather informally, is formally made easier by improved US visa regulations. Other countries in addition to the EU that also prefer international product standards would benefit if within the scope of such an agreement the US abandons national standards. Admittedly, a certain threat of trade diversion with respect to developing countries exists in the case of harmonisation of product standards, primarily because standards would be raised in either the US or the EU. Thus, it would be preferable to mutually recognise standards and to refrain from implementing restrictive origin rules (Langhammer et al., 2002; Chen & Mattoo, 2004).

tariff-reduction formula and plurilateral sector-specific initiatives, see section 4.4). The objective would be to render a large part of transatlantic trade duty-free by an ambitious, multilateral abolition of tariffs. This element would be the second part of the transatlantic strategy.

Agreements with developing and emerging countries

If one merely considers the EU's self-interest, the issue is once more the identification of especially important trading partners among the emerging countries (for example, China), which, owing to their high growth in the long term, offer excellent prospects for an expansion of trade relations.

Yet in comparison with the agreements among industrial countries, the typical free trade agreements between industrial and developing countries are possibly more problematic because they lead to discrimination among developing countries with similar export products.

Another point that should be viewed very critically is trade agreements that are primarily motivated by politics or history.[11] Thus, for example, the EU discriminates between the ex-colonies of its member states in the African, Caribbean and Pacific (ACP) countries and those developing countries without a European colonial past. Even from the EU's own perspective, this strategy must be questioned. The trade-off between resources that are invested in negotiations and the additional transaction costs (the regulation jungle) on the one hand and the volume of trade on the other often does not appear reasonable.[12]

---

[11] Also within the scope of the European tariff preference system, tariffs are charged for example on coffee imported from Brazil while Columbian coffee can be imported duty-free to the EU.

[12] With the European Partnership Agreements (EPAs) that form part of its development policy, the EU has initiated a new wave of a different kind of regional free trade agreement. By 2008, the ACP countries of the respective regions should jointly come to an agreement with respect to the EU regarding a free trade agreement. In doing so, the EU and the ACP countries are fulfilling a requirement by the WTO, which considers the current one-sided EU preferences that are only based on historical circumstances to represent a violation of WTO rules and is tolerated only temporarily by means of exceptions (waivers). With the EPAs, the EU is securing significantly improved market access in the relevant markets. Because the markets of the ACP countries are small, however, the consequences of the EPAs on the global economy will be limited. Regarding development policy,

In order to guard against distortions of competition among the developing countries to at least a certain degree, but above all to avoid increasing transaction costs excessively, it would appear sensible for the EU to negotiate with existing regional associations that include several participants. An example of such negotiations is the talks between the EU and MERCOSUR. The beauty of such negotiations lies in the fact that several countries can be included 'in one go' and the same rules apply to all countries (for instance, the same rules of origin). Moreover, distortion of competition among the participating countries is avoided from the start. Admittedly, it is a problem that many developing countries have not established stable free trade agreements or customs unions, but are rather still in the process of setting them up. For example, the stability of MERCOSUR was considerably impaired by Argentina's financial crisis, and the ASEAN countries have not yet completed the ASEAN Free Trade Area. Negotiations with a region that is itself not yet stable are protracted. Often proposals to reduce tariffs take place based on the participating countries' smallest common denominator. So, negotiations with a group of countries are more difficult than with an individual country.

Other countries' agreements with developing countries

From the EU's perspective, a view must be taken of regional trade agreements that differentiates between developing and emerging countries. These countries are increasingly making use of the opportunities for stronger South-South cooperation. Thus, the ASEAN countries in the longer-term will not only introduce duty-free trade among each other, but also with India and China. In Africa, regional cooperation is also growing stronger. Nevertheless, region-spanning South-South initiatives hardly exist.[13]

---

there are certainly risks associated with regional cooperation among developing countries; however, it may partially result in a diversion of trade in favour of the EU and at the expense of other industrial and emerging countries (which can also represent a disadvantage from the perspective of the ACP countries).

[13] An incidental aspect is the Generalised System of Trade Preferences among developing countries initiated by UNCTAD. This system has been set up as a supplement to the traditional preferences of the industrial countries in favour of developing countries. Yet so far its reach has been very limited.

Free trade agreements among the rapidly growing emerging countries – in particular China and regional neighbours – are rightly a cause for great concern in Europe, as given the fast pace of their technological progress the emerging countries, and above all China, are penetrating markets and sectors that up to now were reserved to the industrial countries (Figure 4.2). This economic and technological catching-up process coupled with the integration of regional trade can seriously impair the competitive position of the industrial countries that remain outside this process.

Figure 4.2 China's rising market share of modern manufactured products – Share of global exports (in %)

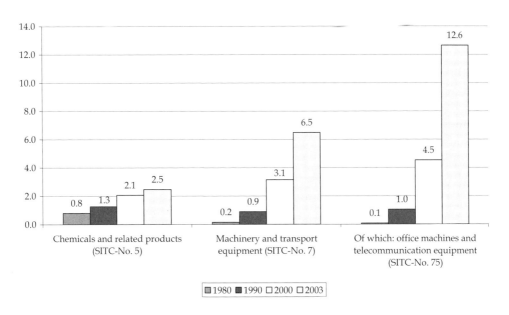

Sources: WTO Statistical Database (retrieved from http://stat.wto.org/Home/ WSDBHome.aspx? Language, 29 November 2004) and authors' calculations.

From the EU's perspective, trade-diverting effects at its expense may yet become considerably larger, because major industrial countries such as Japan and the US are engaged in securing better access to the rapidly growing markets in Asia by means of bilateral agreements.

Consequently, EU trade policy is faced with the challenge of investigating the feasibility of bilateral agreements with the new non-European integration areas, especially in Asia. With the Trans-Regional

EU-ASEAN Trade Initiative, the first attempts in this regard have been made. Also, in recent times calls for the conclusion of a free trade agreement with ASEAN and other important Asian countries can more frequently be heard from German political and industrial circles.[14]

All in all, the EU must accept as a given the trend towards increasingly strong regionalisation of global trade – it cannot reverse it politically. Such acceptance is particularly pertinent in view of the fact that the EU itself is the classic example of a deep and successful regional integration process, and for decades has been managing its trade relations with third countries by means of a large number of bilateral agreements. Certainly, the argument is appropriate that regionalisation curtails the pressure on the WTO process to achieve results in negotiations and can reduce the willingness of WTO members to compromise.

Still, in its own economic interest the EU should in future bear in mind the possibilities of bilateral and regional agreements.[15] If the EU decides to engage in new bilateral agreements, it should make good use of the manifold opportunities that go beyond dismantling tariffs (such as the reduction of non-tariff barriers to trade and progress with issues such as services and standards, along with questions of investment and competition). Agreements are only sensible with economically-relevant trading partners. This rationale means that bilateral agreements are called for that lead to profound and economically relevant integration – and, as far as possible, these agreements should be concluded with existing regional organisations.

4.4   Plurilateral variants

Plurilateral variants refer to approaches in which a larger number of participating countries – but by no means all WTO members – join an association. Organisationally, plurilateral agreements can be secured independently or under the umbrella of the WTO.

From its fundamental approach, the WTO is a multilateral organisation based on the tenet of the 'same rules for all' and its central legal pillars (the GATT, the GATS and the agreement concerning

---

[14] In response to this challenge, from the entrepreneur's perspective foreign direct investment would appear an attractive option for bypassing trade barriers.

[15] For a relativisation of this self-serving perspective, see section 4.5.

intellectual property, the TRIPS) are binding for all WTO members. In principle, a country that joins the WTO cannot be exempt from individual agreements (for example, by applying the GATT, but not the TRIPS). Still, there are some agreements that are optional for WTO members, for example the Government Procurement Agreement, which only 28 WTO members have joined. The rights and duties arising from these agreements only apply to members. In other words, only parties to the agreement grant each other non-discriminatory access to their government procurement markets. This agreement is an exception to the principle of most-favoured nation (MFN) treatment. At the same, all WTO members have the option to join the agreement. It is therefore not a private club, but rather an open entity. This feature satisfies an important requirement that was derived from the theoretical analysis (see chapter 3, section 3.2). A key advantage of a plurilateral agreement under the umbrella of the WTO lies in the fact that during negotiations there is already a high degree of transparency, and all members have the opportunity to take part. Further, all WTO members must approve the agreement – even those that do not wish to join. This stipulation ensures that the agreement does not put countries that are not involved at a disadvantage against their will.

The large advantage of such negotiations is that plurilateral agreements can be concluded even if some WTO members assert reservations against specific regulatory areas. This flexibility applies, for example, to the issues of investment and competition. A range of developing countries oppose multilateral rules for these issues because they would not like to restrict their policy space and do not see any immediate benefits of such rules for themselves.

From the point of view of the negotiations, the borders between plurilateral and multilateral approaches are fluid, because within the scope of multilateral negotiations not all (by far) WTO members actively take part. Rather, four groups of WTO members can generally be distinguished: First are those members that have independent positions and actively take part in negotiations. Second are those members that assume the role of representative for a group of countries. Third is the group that consists of countries that during negotiations let themselves largely be represented by another country. Fourth is the group that consists of countries that take part in the negotiations not by having an independent position, but by judging the final result of the negotiations (and, in the absence of any own particular interests, generally agree). In this regard, multilateral negotiations are actually *de facto* plurilateral as well. Indeed, the term 'plurilateral negotiations' is used in cases in which some countries that normally actively participate in the multilateral process of negotiations do not take part for political reasons.

Another major advantage is that these agreements can be made subject to WTO dispute settlement, which is an effective system of enforcement. This link ensures that the agreements do not contain simple recommendations, but binding rules.

Tariffs

Plurilateral sector initiatives for the entire removal of tariffs in important sectors are very attractive from the perspective of economics. Nevertheless, a key tactical aspect is to avoid weakening negotiations regarding multilateral tariff reductions by conducting parallel activities.

The modalities of the WTO round for dismantling tariffs have as a basis a general tariff-reduction formula that should be applied to all non-agricultural sectors. In addition, sector-specific options are permitted that exceed the general formula's extent of tariff reduction. In this regard, the modalities contain a plurilateral component that should be used. Plurilateral initiatives for the abolition of industrial tariffs in individual sectors are therefore compatible with the Doha Round. There are models for this already: the 1996 Information Technology Agreement (ITA) is a plurilateral agreement that specifies duty-free trade in information technology (IT) products. In the context of this agreement, the realisation that nearly the entire trade in IT products is conducted by a relatively small number of WTO members, and that trade with this innovative sector should not be restricted by tariffs, played a crucial role. The agreement came into force after it was signed by countries that in total represent more than 90% of the international trade in IT products. The Medical Agreement, which stipulates duty-free entry for medical products, coincided with the establishment of the WTO. The background to this agreement is related to development policy (no restriction of trade in products of vital importance). Both agreements have a plurilateral group of members that grant exemption from duties on pertinent products for all WTO members, making this approach particularly attractive.[16]

---

[16] Within the scope of the WTO round, the objective is to negotiate with a view to removing tariffs on environmental goods. Such an agreement could also be plurilateral.

Along the lines of the ITA, for example, the OECD countries in particular could agree to completely dismantle tariffs in those industries in which the countries involved dominate global trade. These tariff reductions would be 'given' to the remaining WTO members by way of MFN treatment. For every segment of industry one could determine a specific threshold value from which the agreement becomes effective (a critical mass of participants). If, for instance, the participating countries do not represent 80, 85 or 90% of global trade (such as is the case with the ITA), tariffs would not be reduced. This threshold would prevent important actors in the respective markets from taking a free-rider position as exporters by profiting from tariff reductions in the partner countries without providing anything in exchange.

The potential for these solutions is substantial. Figure 4.3 shows that the OECD countries (including EU-25 countries that are not OECD members) have a share in world exports with many modern manufactured products exceeding 85% (at times even by a significant margin).[17] This level also applies, for instance, to chemical products, different types of machinery, as well as (above all) road vehicles and other transport equipment.

This approach mainly concerns industrial sectors that exhibit intensive intra-industrial trade in which tariffs play only a minor role (see section 4.2). Admittedly, a plurilateral reduction of tariffs would lead to a competitive disadvantage for those industries and commodities that exhibit a high input of raw materials and in which OECD countries likewise have a very large market share. From the industrial countries' perspective, these effects might be impossible to absorb (section 4.2). Consequently, a sector-wide dismantling of tariffs is improbable.

---

[17] Since the export interests of the countries concerned are the main driving forces of trade agreements and foreclosure *vis-à-vis* imports by means of tariffs as discussed earlier, it does not make sense in the case of modern manufactured products; thus only exports and not the entire trade are considered here. In addition, it is noteworthy that about 80% of exports from the OECD countries are exported to other OECD countries; consequently, internal trade within the OECD is very significant.

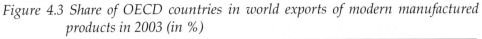

Figure 4.3 Share of OECD countries in world exports of modern manufactured products in 2003 (in %)

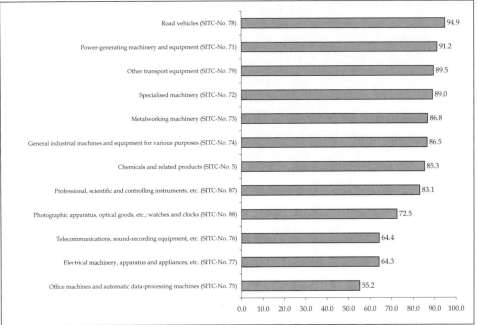

Notes: In this context, the OECD includes EU member states that are not members of OECD. Classification of product groups is in accordance with the Standard International Trade Classification (SITC - Rev. 3).

Sources: OECD, UN and authors' calculations.

With a view to the countries that are not included and which could adopt a free-rider position, one must consider that in the EU, the least-developed countries enjoy exemption from duties and more advanced countries enjoy a partial exemption from duties. These 'gifts' that are granted to free-riding developing countries do not amount to the tariff for MFNs, but to the preferential tariff. At the same time, importers and customs administrations are freed of bureaucratic expenses (determination of the country of origin).

In addition, as argued in section 4.2, one can expect those countries that are not included at least in the medium and long term to continue to liberalise unilaterally. Therefore, a plurilateral initiative on the part of the industrial countries would not fix into perpetuity the tariffs of the non-participating developing countries.

At first glance, achieving a minimum threshold value of (for instance) 90% of the market share of the countries involved would represent a key difficulty with this liberalisation approach, because this group of countries would in some sectors include some larger emerging countries that as a rule charge higher tariff rates on the products concerned. Here, one could assume that these countries might refuse to entirely dismantle tariffs because they would not be receiving any corresponding quid pro quo from the OECD countries in which tariff rates are substantially lower. This argument can be qualified, however. Provided that the OECD area represents the main market of the emerging countries concerned, in their own interest they should contribute to achieving critical mass. In addition, tariffs should in the medium term be dispensable as a protection against competition for the country's own industry (strategic trade policy tariff) – at least where the country has such a high global market share that it belongs to the group of larger exporters. But of course, in the end, the decision about participating in a sector-specific plurilateral agreement from the point of view of the larger emerging countries remains an individual choice that will be examined in each particular case.

It is problematic that sector initiatives could dilute ambitions for a general tariff reduction at the WTO level by way of a formula. For these reasons, sector initiatives should be substantiated only when the Doha Round has led to an agreement about a general tariff-reduction formula.

'New' trade issues

Some of the new WTO issues concern rules that do not fit into the classical trade policy pattern of concession and counter-concession. Thus, for example, the modernisation of customs procedures leads to benefits for all countries involved in international trade. The creation of a functioning competition policy is an essential component of a working market economy. In this respect, it is tolerable if not all WTO members go along with these issues in negotiations – the leading countries' negotiating position for the remaining issues is not weakened (for example, regarding tariffs).

Admittedly, plurilateral agreements are also possible outside the WTO framework. They can be concluded independently of international organisations or be integrated into existing organisational frameworks. One example of such an agreement that some countries were trying to achieve under the OECD umbrella is the Multilateral Agreement on Investment

(MAI). In comparison with the group of WTO members, the OECD countries are economically and politically homogeneous, so that it should be relatively easier to bring about joint rules. At the same time, the example of the MAI points out the drawbacks of rule-setting outside the WTO context (Box 4.1). The non-participating countries are excluded to a much greater extent from the negotiations and cannot veto the establishment of the agreement. These aspects can quickly lead to distrust and suspicions that rules might be agreed that would put third countries at a disadvantage.

Box 4.1 The failed negotiations concerning an MAI under the umbrella of the OECD

The negotiations about a multilateral investment agreement began within the OECD framework in September 1995. The MAI was to provide for legal security for the initial investment phase as well as the operating phase of investments (post-establishment). This attempt was far-reaching in its effort to introduce a top-down approach according to which participating countries would have assured compliance with basic principles such as the non-discrimination of investors and would have only explicitly stipulated exceptions to this basic rule. Additionally, an investor–state dispute settlement system was envisaged. The negotiations that were managed by experts and at first went unnoticed were increasingly criticised in the course of 1997 by non-governmental organisations and parliamentarians from OECD countries. The main allegation was that the MAI talks were being conducted as secret negotiations without any democratic legitimacy and threatened to undermine the sovereignty of the states. Also, public resistance on the part of the parliaments of some countries grew so strong that the governments agreed in early 1998 to discontinue the negotiations. At the end of 1998, France declared that it would not take part in resuming the talks. Thus, the MAI finally failed (Böhmer, 1998).

This side effect leads to the question of whether a plurilateral initiative concerning *investment rules*, which has not made headway in the WTO round, might not lead to considerable political resistance and endanger the entire round. It must be also taken into account that the discussions concerning a WTO investment agreement were characterised by irrational, polemic disputes. These had little to do with the actual contents of a possible agreement and did not deal with the concrete EU proposals, but employed threatening scenarios and even conspiracy theories. With this in mind, one can assume that similar opposition would materialise against a plurilateral agreement. In the case of negotiations under the WTO umbrella, consequences for the WTO round would be conceivable. As to negotiations within the OECD framework, one would have to reckon with opposition. Therefore, after a careful consideration of the advantages and disadvantages of such an agreement, one can arrive at the conclusion that for current political reasons it would be inopportune to take up negotiations. In addition, there are already many bilateral investment agreements (as previously mentioned, see chapter 3, section 3.6) that at least regulate questions of investment protection.

Such strong political opposition is not to be expected in the case of a *competition agreement*. The markets of many WTO members are too small to play an important international role in competition policy. Therefore, for economic reasons it is not necessarily required to include all WTO members in a competition agreement. Moreover, positive effects on third countries can arise from competition rules that are agreed among certain countries if for instance export cartels are dissolved. As a basic principle, for reasons of efficiency the agreed competition rules should be of benefit not only to the members but also to all third countries.

Under these conditions there is no reason not to conclude a plurilateral competition agreement in which predominantly the OECD countries participate. Of course, the parallel objective would have to be to get the most important emerging countries to accede. In order for this to happen, however, a lot of countries – especially the emerging Asian countries – must still be convinced of the advantages of improved rules of competition within the scope of a plurilateral agreement.

By contrast, there is little reason to conclude a plurilateral transparency agreement regarding *government procurement*. The agreement that was originally intended to be multilateral had the objective of bringing countries closer to joining the Government Procurement Agreement (GPA) by way of fundamental rules of transparency. Since plurilateral membership would largely be limited to the countries that are participating in the GPA – and these countries have already entered more far-reaching obligations – such an agreement is superfluous.

Plurilateral agreements only with industrial countries?

The question arises as to whether the EU should follow up these new issues plurilaterally within the WTO framework with a large number of members or mainly with industrial countries within OECD. A key issue is whether action is required among the countries involved. In any case, the question of whether a plurilateral agreement is sensible requires a thorough analysis of the relations between partner countries. Thus, for example, protection of investments and liberalisation for foreign direct investment are by far less pressing problems in OECD countries than in developing and emerging countries. A multilateral investment agreement with the latter would presumably not entail much more than certain basic rules (transparency and non-discrimination). For a plurilateral agreement among OECD countries, this would be a very modest objective. Although a plurilateral competition agreement that included many members from the group of developing countries as well might merely determine the establishment of competition authorities and certain basic rules, a plurilateral agreement among the industrial countries could contain much more detailed definitions that take into account the stage of development of the countries involved. Within the OECD, such an agreement would primarily concern harmonisation of the provisions of competition law, common notification mechanisms, time limits and strengthened cooperation.

In this respect, plurilateral agreements do not have to represent the second-best solution in the sense that parties try to assert their objectives – which were originally multilateral – in a smaller group. Rather, they can offer an opportunity to reconsider the objective and to enhance their ambitions. Of course, thereby one tends to curtail the probability that non-members become parties to the agreement at a later date. But the enlargement of plurilateral agreements – as shown by the example of the GPA – is in any case a political process that is difficult to assess.

Depending on the issue that is to be advanced in such plurilateral agreements, pros and cons must be weighed:

- A far-reaching agreement among OECD countries makes sense if there still is an appreciable need for liberalisation, and with a view to emerging and developing countries, in the nearer future a comprehensive WTO agreement cannot be expected. In this case, it would not be reasonable to downgrade objectives concerning plurilateral agreements in view of their ability to be extended.

- Yet to the extent that among OECD countries extensive liberalisation has already taken place, and deficits merely exist in emerging and developing countries, it makes more sense to conclude a less far-reaching agreement that at least some of these countries can join.

- Moreover, in the final analysis, the question arises as to whether for new issues it is not also possible to agree on two different stages of agreement – a far-reaching one and a rather rudimentary one. But this approach has so far not been successful with respect to the issue of governmental procurement because of opposition on the part of the developing countries against even a rudimentary agreement.

A 'WTO of two speeds' is possibly the only chance for making headway in negotiations on important new issues (on competition and in the longer term also investment and other issues). In this respect, the paradigm that has been upheld since the founding of the WTO should be reviewed, according to which all agreements should be basically binding for all WTO members.

4.5 Recommendations for EU trade policy

Despite the difficulties of the WTO process described above, the multilateral trade order rightly enjoys priority. From the EU perspective, this should continue to be the case, since substantial liberalisation within the WTO framework results in significantly larger welfare gains than regional agreements. Simultaneously, with the help of further multilateral liberalisation, the EU can reduce the trade diversion it suffers because of regional trade agreements among other countries. For the same reason, the EU should work towards strengthening the WTO rules for regional trade agreements (as discussed in chapter 3, section 3.4 and chapter 5).

Taking into account the view that the removal of tariffs is fundamentally in the EU's self-interest, but that a unilateral liberalisation would be politically disadvantageous with regard to the mercantilist quid-pro-quo approach of the WTO negotiations, a plurilateral approach would be best suited to strongly reduce the EU's tariffs. The EU should pioneer the sectoral elimination of tariffs. This approach exceeds the general tariff reduction (formula) within the WTO framework and is compatible with the modalities of the Doha Round. In doing so, a critical mass of participating countries should be specified on a sector-by-sector basis, which taken together represents a very high proportion of global trade. Tariff reduction on the basis of MFN treatment would be 'given' to the remaining countries (as was the case with the ITA).

Given the large number of bilateral agreements that have been concluded in the recent past, chapter 3 shows that this *might* constitute a problem for the WTO and for the smooth functioning of global trade. The EU's self-serving ambition for more bilateral associations may conflict with the multilateral solution. Thus the question arises as to how far the EU, as one of the largest actors in the global economy, should subordinate its interests to the higher objective of the world trading order and assume a model function to motivate other countries to show stronger discipline concerning regionalism.

This argument - in conjunction with the one about transaction costs and the fact that the limited capacities for negotiations must be used as effectively as possible - results in the demand for restraint with regard to further bilateral trade agreements. As far as the EU is pondering whether to start new negotiations (as otherwise its interests would suffer too severely), it should take into account a range of criteria:

- The trading partner(s) concerned should be economically significant and exhibit dynamic economic development.

- To the extent possible, negotiations should be conducted with a group of countries that have already agreed free trade among themselves. That way, trade distortions among these countries are avoided.

- The objective of the agreement should be deep economic integration. In addition to tariffs and import quotas, this concerns the liberalisation of trade in services, which should be as comprehensive as possible, as well as the incorporation of new trade issues (investment, competition, trade facilitation, government procurement and improved regulatory collaboration).

- In the transatlantic relationship, owing to the close investment relations there are very specific problems that to a great extent relate to the issue of regulatory collaboration (cooperation between authorities and legislatures). At the same time, the EU and the US bear a large political responsibility for the multilateral trade system. Thus, it appears sensible to regulate technical questions of the bilateral economic relationship within the scope of a transatlantic trade and investment agreement, and to continue to pursue the reduction of tariffs under the auspices of the WTO.

Regarding new trade issues, it is reasonable for the EU to pursue plurilateral solutions, and to decide on a case-by-case basis whether deep integration among OECD countries or a rather rudimentary integration that includes a number of emerging countries (or both) is considered appropriate.

5. Conclusions

The slow pace of the WTO negotiations and the rapid increase of regional trade agreements since the mid-1990s raise the question of which approaches the EU should choose from among the range of available trade policy options (unilateral, bilateral, plurilateral or multilateral, or a combination of these). Is the Lamy doctrine – which gives highest priority to the WTO process while imposing a moratorium on entering into new negotiations on bilateral deals – the best solution?

A survey of the development of regional trade agreements shows that since the 1990s and especially since the turn of the millennium a new phase has emerged with a hitherto unknown dynamism. According to the WTO, in 2005 about half of global trade has occurred within such associations. This finding underlines the point that EU trade policy is faced with a substantial worldwide trend that must not be ignored.

The strong dominance of bilateral agreements between two countries is remarkable and new. These constitute about 90% of the agreements concluded since 1995 and reported to the WTO up to May 2004.[1] The agreements often involve countries that develop to become a 'hub' with numerous 'spokes'. This model can be seen to apply to a number of countries such as the US, Mexico, Chile and some Asian countries, which in the past exclusively or to a very large extent subscribed only to the multilateral negotiating process. Yet recently, these countries have been actively turning to bilateral or regional trade agreements and emulating the pioneer of this approach – the EU.

---

[1] As a result of the EU's eastern enlargement, more than 60 regional trade agreements have lapsed, of which a large proportion was concluded after 1995.

Additional dimensions of this new phase of regionalism are the greater scope of a series of agreements that more often than previously go beyond the pure dismantling of tariffs and include issues such as services and investment, but without aiming at deeper integration such as economic and monetary unions as was partly the case with earlier associations. In addition, there are indications that in the long term, continent-spanning regional trade zones could develop in Europe (including the Mediterranean region), America, Asia and Africa, which could become interconnected by way of some trade agreements among individual countries or country groups.

The rising momentum to conclude regional trade agreements is partly related to political motives (for example, peacekeeping or political stability), but often a whole range of important economic reasons as well. Primarily, this includes the hope for increases in welfare through a stronger international division of labour. From a mercantilist perspective, what is also associated with this trend is that regional trade agreements facilitate or protect access to foreign markets for a country's own export industry. In this respect, there are signs of a certain degree of competition between the EU and the US (and partly Japan) over emerging countries that represent attractive markets – for instance with respect to Chile, Mexico and MERCOSUR as well as the East-Asian region. Especially from the view of developing and emerging countries, market access and market protection is likewise a main motive for the frequent agreements with industrial nations in their region. Moreover, in regionalisation these countries see an opportunity to underpin (lock-in) the credibility of their structural reforms and to attract foreign investors.[2] In the age of globalisation, regional trade agreements provide the opportunity for the industrial nations to turn countries in their neighbourhood into 'extended workbenches' for outsourcing labour-intensive production steps and then re-importing the processed goods duty-free, instead of producing them in their own country as before. The stagnating WTO process is certainly another cause for the dynamism of regionalisation, but is by no means decisive by itself.

---

[2] This trend also means that developing countries as a rule no longer use regional trade agreements as they often did in the 1960s and 1970s, with the purpose of protecting themselves against third countries in the context of an import-substitution policy.

Regarding the welfare effects of regional trade agreements, two basic effects must be weighed against one another from the perspective of an individual country. The positive effect of trade creation stems from the fact that by reducing barriers to trade with respect to the partner country, domestic products are substituted by cheaper goods from the partner country. The negative effect of trade diversion is caused by the fact that possibly more efficient suppliers from non-member countries that are discriminated against by the association are replaced by competitors from the partner country who are more expensive and can only 'artificially' offer goods and services at a lower price owing to the agreement. Seen from a global perspective, this situation can lead to ineffective specialisation and a questionable allocation of resources. The net welfare effect of regional trade agreements remains ambiguous – even when new developments of international trade theory are considered. This point applies to an individual country's perspective as well as to a global view that takes the disadvantages to third countries into account.

The picture looks somewhat brighter for those trade agreements that cover domestic regulations. Here it has been shown that the theoretical welfare effects from an individual country's perspective are clearly positive, as a diversion of trade does not occur; instead a reduction of real resource costs takes place, which empirically tends to be non-negligible. From a global perspective, however, third countries are again put at a disadvantage and an agreement can therefore easily lead to a misallocation of resources.

Empirical studies of traditional regional trade agreements do not offer ultimate clarity either. Therein, most regional agreements increase the welfare of the countries involved to a limited degree, but partly lead to trade-diverting effects at the expense of third countries. Generalisations are hardly possible; in the end, it depends on the individual case. The total global welfare effects are disclosed in virtually none of the studies and therefore continue to remain largely unclear. Nevertheless, the associations are usually not characterised by foreclosure with respect to third countries. Nor is the establishment of trade blocs that are motivated by protectionism (trade fortresses) on the horizon. External protection is not systematically increased in the course of regionalisation – not least because of the GATT rules – and at times it is even diminished.

In the final analysis, however, some general statements can be derived about how trade creation can be augmented, how trade diversion can be reduced and thus how the likelihood for positive welfare effects can be increased. For instance, this is more likely to be the case:

- the greater the cost differences are between the partner countries and the lower these are between members and non-members;

- the higher the tariffs initially were among the partner countries and the lower they are determined to be after concluding the agreement with respect to non-members; and

- the more open an association is for accession by those third countries that possibly feel disadvantaged.

Further, it must be borne in mind that the large number of overlapping trade agreements (the 'spaghetti bowl phenomenon') raises the transaction costs of global trade and has the effect of 'sand in the wheels'. This outcome is considerably reinforced by complicated rules of origin.

In addition, individual countries have a strong incentive to react to agreements on the part of their trading partners by concluding their own agreements in order to minimise trade-diverting effects at their expense. This response can easily result in a self-reinforcing process, which we call 'a race for markets'. Theoretically, this process is associated with negative external effects, so one can assume that the trend towards regionalisation is too pronounced for the global economy overall. From a game-theoretical point of view, bilateralism is a dominant strategy and leads to a kind of 'prisoner's dilemma'. More specifically, for the individual actors it is always rational to conclude bilateral agreements – independent of the behaviour of the remaining trading partners. If the competitors do not conclude an agreement with an interesting country it is best for the individual country to do so and thus to gain a competitive advantage. If, however, the competing countries themselves go ahead with this strategy, the individual country is forced to follow in order to achieve a level playing field again. Individual and collective rationality therefore diverge because individual countries do not take global welfare into account.

The proliferation of bilateral agreements in the course of an exaggerated race for markets entails the possibility that global welfare is impaired for the following reasons:

- In line with an increasingly complex network of bilateral agreements, the transaction costs of global trade inexorably continue to rise.

- Some of the new bilateral trade agreements that have been concluded in the race for markets could on their own lead to negative global welfare effects.

- The more often developing countries conclude a North-South agreement with a particular industrial country, the more the danger grows that the developing countries cannot achieve the expected welfare gains. Rather, welfare losses can occur because in the end, access to the industrial country's market is a positional good whose value decreases as the number of participants increases.

In order to prevent such a scenario, multilateral cooperation would be necessary, in which all countries would have to agree to abstain from a race for markets. Such cooperation is problematic, however, because an agreement in favour of global welfare is, in the end, a global public good. Even if the incentives for the individual countries are hardly compelling, the WTO is nevertheless the suitable forum for such coordination.[3]

Regionalisation does not necessarily mean that the WTO must accept a loss of significance. Despite regionalisation, the WTO's rules and dispute settlement mechanism remain a backbone of global trade. There are also aspects of regionalism that can be conducive to the WTO process, such as countries becoming accustomed to their international competition, and, in the case of the 'new trade issues', there is potential for learning (i.e. a laboratory phase for subsequent multilateral solutions such as elementary rules for competition policy). In addition, negotiations at the multilateral level can hardly be disturbed by bilateral trade agreements concerning a key area: the reduction of EU agricultural subsidies, which would benefit all countries that export agricultural goods. For the EU there is no incentive to make this concession in bilateral negotiations, because it would then receive substantially less in exchange in the form of improved market access for its export industries than in the multilateral context.

There are nevertheless some strong indications that the WTO negotiations are suffering from regionalisation – meaning that regional

---

[3] The WTO (and the GATT) can absolutely be seen as being such a forum, since basically the incentive exists for large countries to improve their own terms of trade by imposing (high) tariffs at the expense of the rest of the world. Nevertheless, the threat of a trade war exists if other large countries take retaliatory measures. In the context of binding global trade rules at the WTO level, large countries are exercising self-restraint.

agreements represent stumbling blocks for multilateral agreement. For example, the pressure to agree falls if attractive trade policy alternatives exist or if important markets of the export industry have already been or are expected to be opened by bilateral agreements. There are some indications that this is already the case in the current Doha negotiations. Moreover, restricted negotiation capacities can be tied up by negotiating bilateral agreements. A further important aspect is that regional trade agreements establish benefits that can lead to opposition against the multilateral liberalisation of trade because a general tariff reduction lowers the 'artificial' advantage with respect to third countries (preference erosion). Generally, the more influential the politically-favoured export industry is, the more the multilateral process slows down. Currently, numerous developing countries that have preferential access to the markets of the industrial countries (among others, the African, Caribbean and Pacific or ACP countries and the least-developed countries) are currently delaying progress in the Doha Round because they see entire economic structures in their countries at stake. This situation represents a striking example of specific regional trade arrangements having led to a questionable allocation of resources.

In the context of these diverse interests, the question arises as to how the WTO should in future deal with regionalism, because fundamentally, the WTO has the task of setting generally applicable rules for the regionalisation process. This matter is one of primarily limiting the negative impact on non-member countries (trade diversions) and curtailing excessive regionalisation (transaction costs). The basic rules of Art. XXIV of the GATT, particularly the requirements to liberalise "substantially all the trade" and not to increase external barriers represent a good foundation. Nevertheless, the WTO rules should be specified and tightened.

- For instance, despite foreseeable strong resistance, a requirement should be introduced to reduce trade barriers with respect to third countries when establishing regional agreements.

- The WTO review mechanism also needs to be strengthened to better supervise compliance with the rules. For this to occur, it is necessary to add legally unequivocal interpretations to a range of unclear wordings in Art. XXIV of the GATT. For example, the exact meaning of the requirement to include "substantially all trade" in a regional trade agreement needs to be clarified.

- In addition, it would be sensible to limit the sharp rise in transaction costs stemming from the spaghetti bowl effect in conjunction with highly complicated rules of origin. Hence, the preferential rules of origin should be harmonised under the auspices of the WTO in order to create more uniformity and transparency.

The WTO is fundamentally the suitable forum for coordination and consultation regarding regional agreements with the objective of curbing an uncontrolled race for markets. But it is not a realistic framework for these aims without the vigorous commitment on the part of important actors. Another core point in the context of the WTO's Doha Round is to substantially lower tariffs within the most-favoured nation (MFN) treatment, in order to render regional trade agreements less attractive.

From the perspective of developing countries, South-South agreements in principle provide the opportunity for welfare gains, primarily by an increased use of economies of scale and more international competition. Yet when small and rather poor developing countries establish an association, there is a threat of a strong diversion of trade and an ineffective allocation of resources. To prevent the associated welfare losses from the view of the individual country, in these cases it is also necessary to lower the barriers to trade *vis-à-vis* third countries. From the vantage point of developing countries, North-South agreements offer more benefits than South-South ones. These benefits include access to larger markets and thereby also the greater use of economies of scale, increased competitive pressure, less diversion of trade, more transfer of technology, a possible lock-in of reforms as well as a rise in foreign direct investment. But in the case of agreements with large industrial countries, developing countries often have to accept that they must liberalise to a greater extent than their partners and agree to certain environmental and social standards. Furthermore, with North-South regionalism, the danger exists that smaller developing countries, which as markets are not so interesting for industrial nations, fall by the wayside.

Regional agreements provide the opportunity to agree on regulations regarding trade issues, with which for political reasons no progress can be achieved within the scope of the WTO. For instance, the opposition among WTO members against a multilateral investment agreement can hardly be overcome. The WTO is not even capable of consensus regarding the objective of creating international rules for competition. The need for regulation of these areas is becoming increasingly urgent in view of the growing importance of foreign direct investment and the proliferating integration among national markets. Another field for pragmatic bilateral and regional cooperation concerns questions of practical collaboration on technical regulations and politically sensitive issues concerning international trade in services (for example, the bilateral recognition of diplomas, etc.). Although with these issues the non-discriminatory multilateral rules under the auspices of the WTO would be ideal, one can also find within the scope of bilateral agreements meaningful regulations that limit possible diversions of trade. Therefore, regional agreements should aim at deepening economic integration. In the longer term, the opportunity exists that different models of regional associations will begin to compete with one another on an institutional level and that the arrangement that in the end appears most suitable might serve as a framework for future WTO rules.

In the second part of this study, options are presented for EU trade policy mainly from the perspective of the EU's self-interest. The most important conclusion is that for the EU, the WTO should continue to have the highest priority, because the EU would profit most from multilateral liberalisation. Without the EU's commitment to opening markets in the agricultural sector, the Doha Round cannot succeed. According to this reasoning, the EU cannot expect a free ride from a successful multilateral process but must make its own substantial contribution. This point is not only true for the traditional negotiations on tariffs but also for the refining of WTO rules concerning regional agreements and antidumping, and for establishing a binding agreement on trade facilitation. The key role of the EU is particularly evident with regard to the honing of the rules that govern regional trade agreements. As a historical driving force of regionalisation, the EU could do this credibly if it issues demands that would represent a significant need for the EU to adapt as well. This approach particularly concerns the harmonisation of preferential rules of origin. The EU has to bear in mind that it is indeed a key player with a crucial impact on the negotiations.

Within the scope of its trade strategy, the EU should consider that its tariffs possess no economic justification in most manufacturing sectors. Customs revenues are out of all proportion to the associated administrative expenses, while the level of tariffs is so low that they do not effectively protect domestic industry. Further, efforts within the scope of a strategic trade policy are not very effective, for theoretical reasons alone. In this context the costs of the customs administration must also be considered – the most evident one being the salaries of customs officers – along with the costs of customs handling procedures borne by manufacturers, merchants, forwarders and finally consumers. Statistically each customs officer generates annual revenue of only €85,000. This figure is clear evidence of the fact that customs revenue is disproportionate to the administrative costs involved. Under these circumstances tariffs are pointless.

In view of these facts, the EU would do itself a favour for purely economic reasons if it were to unilaterally abolish tariffs in most industries. This recommendation is less starry-eyed than it may appear at first sight, since empirically, the unilateral dismantling of tariffs – usually as an element of a broader design for economic reform – represents by far the most important form of liberalisation that has occurred in developing countries during the last two decades. Admittedly, however, a unilateral reduction of tariffs has the key disadvantage of losing bargaining chips for counter-concessions during international negotiations. For that reason, the EU will probably prefer to adopt other strategies.

The EU must accept the global trend towards bilateral agreements as a given. Moreover, as has been pointed out, bilateral agreements are generally in the EU's interest, particularly with regard to domestic regulations, where welfare effects are more favourable than in the case of tariffs and where – owing to the complexity of the issue – multilateral progress is very slow.

That being said, bilateral agreements are an option that the EU should pursue with great care. Restraint is sensible in order to limit the rise in the transaction costs of global trade that results from the spaghetti bowl phenomenon. In addition, the EU should set a good example by leading the way and motivating other countries to focus more fully on the WTO round and refrain from an excessive race for markets.

Yet this can only be a temporary assessment. Irregardless of whether the WTO round fails, drags on without any palpable progress or is concluded successfully, the balance of the pros and cons of a moratorium on new bilateral deals will change substantially. Hence, as with all doctrines, the reasoning behind the Lamy doctrine has a limited lifespan. Already companies that are at risk of losing their competitive edge in emerging markets through growing regionalisation are increasingly urging the EU to strengthen bilateral economic relations, particularly with the dynamic Asian economies. Where the responsibility for the demands of the global trade system conflict too strongly with the EU's self-interests, and individual bilateral agreements are essential to avoid being at a significant disadvantage regarding access to important markets, the EU should emphasise quality over quantity and go for more profound integration incorporating new trade issues. Owing to the rise in transaction costs associated with bilateral agreements, only economically significant partners or (where possible) groups of countries should be considered.[4]

With a view to possible bilateral agreements, a transatlantic association with the US appears an obvious choice because of the size of its market. Yet for many policy-makers and academics, a bilateral deal between the EU and the US is considered taboo. They fear that such an agreement would render the multilateral system irrelevant. This predominately political argument can be challenged. For the largest part of transatlantic trade, only very low tariffs exist. Moreover, bilateral exports and imports are marked by intra-company trade, which has proved to be robust despite wide fluctuations in exchange rates. In addition, given the structure of transatlantic trade (mainly capital-intensive), one cannot expect that the products of developing countries (mainly labour-intensive) would lose their competitive edge. The trade-creating and -diverting effects of a bilateral dismantling of tariffs would therefore be rather limited. Still, such a deal would indeed be a strong political signal with possible repercussions for the WTO. In assessing a transatlantic agreement, one must also take account of the fact that the EU and the US bear a key political responsibility for the multilateral trade system.

Problems in transatlantic trade are more persistent in the non-tariff area. These primarily concern the many questions of detail that play a role in the course of the intensive integration that is taking place between the EU and the US through multinational companies and often relate to the regulatory collaboration between authorities. From this perspective, one can derive a strategy for approaching the real problems – namely non-tariff issues (questions of investment, competition policy, services and regulatory cooperation) – through a trade and investment agreement and to exclude

---

[4] The danger with such a strategy, being that primarily poorer developing countries will be sidelined, is diminished by the fact that the EU continues to focus on multilateral liberalisation. This focus means that EU tariff preferences will lose value in comparison with the tariffs associated with the MFN treatment.

tariffs in view of the political responsibility for the multilateral trade order. Hence one would leave the issue of dismantling tariffs to the WTO.

The proposed association would be a so-called 'friendship agreement', dealing mainly with the technical questions of detail mentioned above. Here, trade-diverting effects can as a rule be expected to be rather insignificant. The basic idea of such an agreement lies in giving those issues that were already negotiated in the past in various committees without lasting success more political weight by grouping them within one agreement, providing them with an improved chance of being implemented. Of course, it remains to be seen whether this will be successful.

Apart from the US, emerging markets such as China, India and the ASEAN countries appear to be the most attractive partners for new EU bilateral trade agreements. Free trade agreements with these countries would offer good prospects for trade creation and could be seen as a response to increasing regional integration – particularly in Asia. The advanced Asian countries are increasingly becoming competitors for the EU in the established high technology markets. If these countries grant themselves preferential access to their markets, the EU can thus be put at a significant disadvantage. This development requires a response on the part of the EU – at least in the medium term.

Plurilateral approaches, being a middle ground between bilateral deals and multilateral solutions, lend themselves as a flexible and effective 'third way'. They allow like-minded countries to set up rules that go beyond the general WTO context. Plurilateral agreements should preferably be concluded within the WTO, thus allowing all WTO members to observe the negotiations and giving them the opportunity to join during the negotiations or after the establishment of an agreement. The EU should explore the viability of this approach in detail.

A convincing area for a plurilateral approach – and an alternative to a transatlantic dismantling of tariffs – is an initiative for the sectoral elimination of tariffs. The OECD countries could offer the elimination of tariffs in those industries in which a large share of global trade is conducted by the industrial countries. A prerequisite for this move is the definition of a share in global trade that the signatory countries must together represent for the agreement to come into force (for example, 85 or 90%). In many industrial sectors, OECD countries account for more than 85% of world trade. The plurilateral approach would mean that a reduction of tariffs would simply be 'given' to the non-participating countries. A crucial challenge of this method may be to discourage fast-growing developing countries from seeking a free ride and to instead take part the agreement. The political support of many industrial sectors in OECD countries probably depends on whether China and India would join the tariff-dismantling efforts. Still, one has to keep in mind that the relevance of unilateral tariff elimination on the part of these emerging countries must not be underestimated.

The Information Technology Agreement provides a model for this approach. Using this sectoral, 'plurilateral tariff-reduction initiative' one could free transatlantic trade in the key EU industries from tariffs without generating trade distortion with the other OECD countries and the developing countries – as would be the case with a transatlantic association between the EU and the US. In addition, inclusion in the WTO framework also permits a high degree of transparency and a certain say in the matter for third countries. Admittedly, timing is critical. Sectoral tariff-reduction initiatives could reduce the pressure to agree on an ambitious general tariff-reduction formula within the scope of the WTO round. Therefore, this approach should perhaps be pursued only as a second step, after a general tariff-reduction formula has been agreed.

Plurilateral initiatives are also advisable for the various new trade issues (competition policy, standards and in the longer term, investment) where a multilateral approach is currently not achieving any progress. But again, timing will be a decisive factor. At present it is difficult to imagine that a plurilateral investment agreement could be negotiated in the WTO without stirring up fierce and highly emotional debates. A plurilateral competition agreement would probably face less resistance. The question could be posed, however, whether negotiating capacities should be tied up and attention distracted from the Doha Round, given the fragile state of these negotiations. Yet, for a fresh start on these issues the EU would have to rethink its objectives and plurilateral agreements offer the opportunity to be much more ambitious compared with a multilateral approach.

The paradigm that was enshrined when the WTO was founded, whereby all agreements should be basically binding for all WTO members, should be reviewed. A two-tiered WTO may turn out be the only possible way to move the world trading system forward. The EU is well advised to prepare to lead the way to facilitate this development.

REFERENCES

Alexandraki, Katerina and Hans Peter Lankes (2004), *The Impact of Preference Erosion on Middle-Income Developing Countries*, Working Paper No. WP/04/169, IMF, Washington, D.C.

Baier, Scott L. and Jeffrey H. Bergstrand (2004), "Economic Determinants of Free Trade Agreements", *Journal of International Economics*, Vol. 64, pp. 29-63.

Baldwin, Richard E. (1997), "The Causes of Regionalism", *World Economy*, Vol. 20, No. 7, pp. 865-88.

Baldwin, Richard E. and Joseph Francois (1996), "Transatlantic Free Trade: A Quantitative Assessment", mimeo, Centre for Economic Policy Research, London.

Baldwin, Richard E. and Anthony J. Venables (1995), "Regional Economic Integration" in Gene M. Grossman and Kenneth Rogoff (eds), *Handbook of International Economics*, Vol. III, Amsterdam: North Holland, pp. 1597-644.

Baldwin, Richard E. and Charles Wyplosz (2004), *The Economics of European Integration,* Maidenhead: McGraw-Hill.

Bhagwati, Jagdish (1992), "Regionalism versus Multilateralism", *World Economy*, Vol. 15, No. 5, pp. 535-55.

Böhmer, Alexander (1998), "The Struggle for a Multilateral Agreement on Investment: An Assessment of the Negotiation Process in the OECD" in the *German Yearbook of International Law*, Vol. 41, pp. 267-98.

Chen, Maggie Xiaoyang and Aaditya Mattoo (2004), *Regionalism in Standards: Good or Bad for Trade?*, Working Paper No. 3458, World Bank, Washington, D.C.

Corden, Max (1972), "Economies of Scale and Customs Union Theory", *Journal of Political Economy*, Vol. 80, Heft 3, No. 1, pp. 465-75.

Croce, Enzo, V. Hugo Juan-Ramón and Feng Zhu (2004), *Performance of Western Hemisphere Trading Blocs: A Cost-Corrected Gravity Approach*, Working Paper No. WP/04/109, IMF, Washington, D.C.

Davison, Leigh and Debra Johnson (2002), "The EU's Evolving Stance on the International Dimension of Competition Policy: A Critical Commentary", *Intereconomics*, Vol. 37, Book 5, pp. 244-52.

De Santis, Roberto A. (1998), *Trade policy and general equilibrium under different market regimes with numerical applications to Turkey*, University of Warwick.

Dieter, Heribert (2003), *Abschied vom Multilateralismus? Der neue Regionalismus in der Handels- und Finanzpolitik*, SWP-Studie No. 2003/S04, Stiftung Wissenschaft und Politik, Berlin.

———— (2004), *Ursprungsregeln in Freihandelszonen: Protektionismus durch die Hintertür*, SWP-Studie 2004/S09, Stiftung Wissenschaft und Politik, Berlin.

Elliott, Kimberly Ann and Richard B. Freeman (2003), *Can Labour Standards Improve under Globalisation?*, Institute for International Economics, Washington, D.C.

Estevadeordal, Antoni and Kati Suominen (2003), *Measuring Rules of Origin in the World Trading System and Proposals for Multilateral Harmonisation*, paper presented at the APEC Capacity-Building Workshop on Quantitative Methods for Assessing NTMs and Trade Facilitation, Bangkok.

Ethier, Wilfried J. (1998), "The New Regionalism", *The Economic Journal*, Vol. 108, No. 449, pp. 1149-61.

Feinberg, Richard E. (2003), "The Political Economy of United States' Free Trade Agreements", *The World Economy*, Vol. 26, No. 7, pp. 1019-40.

Foroutan, Faezeh (1998), "Does Membership of a Regional Preferential Trade Agreement Make a Country More or Less Protectionist?", *The World Economy*, Vol. 21, No. 3, pp. 305-36.

Fratianni, Michele and John Pattison (2001), "International Organisations in a World of Regional Trade Agreements: Lessons from Club Theory", *The World Economy*, Vol. 24, No. 3, pp. 333-58.

Freund, Caroline (2003), *Reciprocity in Free Trade Agreements*, Policy Research Working Paper No. 3061, World Bank, Washington, D.C.

Glania, Guido (2004), "Various Approaches for Institutional Reform within the WTO", *Aussenwirtschaft*, Vol. 59, No. 1, pp. 7-30.

Graham, Edward M. (2000), "Trade Competition, and the WTO Agenda" in Jeffrey J. Schott (ed.), *The WTO after Seattle*, Institute for International Economics, Washington, D.C.

Hamilton, Daniel S. and Joseph P. Quinlan (2004), *Partners in Prosperity: The Changing Geography of the Transatlantic Economy*, Center for Transatlantic Relations, Washington, D.C.

Hauser, Heinz and Kai-Uwe Schanz (1995), *Das neue GATT: Die Welthandelsordnung nach Abschluss der Uruguay-Runde*, München: Oldenbourg Wiss.

Hilaire, Alvin and Yongzheng Yang (2003), *The United States and the New Regionalism/Bilateralism*, Working Paper No. WP/03/206, IMF, Washington, D.C.

Kaiser, Corinne (2003), *Regionale Integration und das globale Handelssystem*, DVS No. 38, Duisburger Volkswirtschaftliche Schriften, Berlin: Duncker and Humbolt.

Kennes, Walter (2000), *Small Developing Countries and Global Markets: Competing in the Big League*, New York: St. Martin's Press.

Krueger, Anne O. (1999), "Are Preferential Trading Arrangements Trade-Liberalizing or Protectionist?", *Journal of Economic Perspectives*, Vol. 13, No. 4, pp. 105-24.

Krugman, Paul R. (1991), "Is Bilateralism Bad?" in Elhanan Helpman and Assaf Razin (ed.), *International Trade and Trade Policy*, Cambridge, MA: MIT Press, pp. 9-23.

Krugman, Paul R. and Maurice Obstfeld (1997), *International Economics: Theory and Policy*, Reading, MA: Addison-Wesley.

Lamy, Pascal (2002), "Stepping Stones or Stumbling Blocks? The EU's Approach towards the Problem of Multilateralism vs. Regionalism in Trade Policy", *The World Economy*, Vol. 22, No. 10, pp. 1399-413.

Langhammer, Rolf J. and Ludger Wößmann (2002), "Erscheinungsformen regionaler Integrationsabkommen im weltwirtschaftlichen Ordnungsrahmen: Defizite und Dynamik" in Alfred Schüller and Thieme H. Jörg (eds), *Ordnungsprobleme der Weltwirtschaft*, Schriften zu Ordnungsfragen der Wirtschaft, Bd. 71, Stuttgart: Lucius & Lucius Verlags-GmbH, pp. 373-97.

Langhammer, Rolf J., Daniel Piazolo and Horst Siebert (2002), "Assessing Proposals for a Transatlantic Free Trade Area", *Aussenwirtschaft*, Vol. 57, II, pp. 161-85.

Lewis, Jeffrey, Sherman Robinson and Karen Thierfelder (1999), *After the Negotiations: Assessing the Impact of Free Trade Agreements in Southern Africa*, Discussion Paper No. 46, Trade and Macroeconomics Division, International Food Policy Research Institute, Washington, D.C.

Lipsey, Richard (1960), "The Theory of Customs Unions: A General Survey", *The Economic Journal*, Vol. 70, pp. 496-513.

Lloyd, Peter J. (2002), "New Bilateralism in the Asia-Pacific", *The World Economy*, Vol. 26, No. 9, pp. 1279-96.

Lloyd, Peter J. and Donald MacLaren (2003), *The Case of Free Trade and the Role of RTAs*, paper prepared for the Seminar on Regional Trade Agreements and the WTO, 14 Nov. 2003, Geneva.

Matthes, Jürgen (2001), *Neuer Protektionismus? Perspektiven für eine weitere Liberalisierung des Welthandels*, No. 267, Beiträge zur Wirtschafts- und Sozialpolitik, Cologne.

————— (2004), *Entwicklungsländer: Ökonomische Performance und Erfolgsstrategien im Zeitalter der Globalisierung*, No. 6, IW-Analysen, Cologne.

Meade, James E. (1955), *The Theory of Customs Unions*, Amsterdam: North-Holland.

Moïsé, Evdokia (2003), "Rules of Origin" in OECD (ed.), *Regionalism and the Multilateral Trading System*, OECD, Paris, pp. 87-96 and pp. 159-69.

Neary, Peter J. (2004), "Europe on the road to Doha: Towards a new global trade round?", *CESifo Economic Studies*, Vol. 50, No. 2, pp. 319-32.

Nottage, Hunter (2003), "Competition Policy" in OECD (ed.), *Regionalism and the Multilateral Trading System*, OECD, Paris, pp. 71-86.

Organisation for Economic Cooperation and Development (OECD) (2001a), *Regional integration: Observed Trade and Other Economic Effects*, OECD, Paris.

————— (2001b), *Trade and Competition Policies, Options for a Greater Coherence*, OECD, Paris.

Panagariya, Arvind (1999), "The Regionalism Debate: An Overview", *The World Economy*, Vol. 22, No. 4, pp. 455-76.

————— (2000), "Preferential Trade Liberalisation: The Traditional Theory and New Developments", *Journal of Economic Literature*, Vol. 38, June, pp. 287-31.

Petersmann, Ernst-Ulrich (1996), "International Competition Rules for Governments and for Private Business: The Case for Linking Future WTO Negotiations on Investment, Competition and Environmental Rules to Reforms of Anti-Dumping Laws", *Journal of World Trade*, Vol. 30, No. 3, pp. 5-35.

Rose, Andrew K. (2002), *Do WTO Members Have More Liberal Trade Policy?*, Working Paper No. 9347, National Bureau of Economic Research, Cambridge, MA, and the *Journal of International Economics* (forthcoming).

———— (2004), "Do We Really Know that the WTO Increases Trade?", *American Economic Review*, Vol. 94, No. 1, pp. 98-114.

Rose, Klaus and Karlhans Sauernheimer (1999), *Theorie der Aussenwirtschaft*, 13th Auflage, Munich: Verlag Vahlen.

Sapir, André (2000), "Two Tribes", *CEPR European Economic Perspectives*, No. 27, pp. 3-4.

Schiff, Maurice and Alan L. Winters (2002), "Regionalism and Development: The Implications of World Bank Research for ACP and Latin American Countries", *Journal of World Trade*, Vol. 36, No. 3, pp. 479-99.

———— (2003), *Regional Integration and Development*, World Bank, Washington, D.C. and Oxford: Oxford University Press.

Schott, Jeffrey J. (2003), *Competitive Liberalisation: How it Affects the Multilateral Trading System*, paper prepared for the WTO Seminar on Regional Trade Agreements and the WTO, 14 November 2003, Geneva.

———— (ed.) (2004), *Free Trade Agreements: US Strategies and Priorities*, Institute for International Economics, Washington, D.C.

Siebert, Horst (1997), *Weltwirtschaft*, Stuttgart: Lucius & Lucius.

Slaughter, Matthew J. (2003), *Tariff Elimination for Industrial Goods: Why the Gains Will Far Outweigh Any Losses*, background paper prepared for The National Foreign Trade Council, August 2003, Washington, D.C.

Slootmaekers, Veerle (2004), *Trade effects of the EU-Mexico free trade agreement*, Working Papers No. 416, Kiel Institute of World Economics, Kiel.

Soloaga, Isidora and Alan L. Winters (2001), *Regionalism in the 1990s: What Effect on Trade?*, Policy Research Working Paper No. 2156, World Bank, Washington, D.C.

Stern, Robert M. (2003), *Labour Standards and Trade Agreements*, Discussion Paper No. 496, Research Seminar in International Economics, University of Michigan 18 August 2003.

Subramanian, Arvind and Shang-Jin Wei (2003), *The WTO Promotes Trade, Strongly but Unevenly*, Working Paper No. 10024, National Bureau of Economic Research, Cambridge, MA.

United States Trade Representative (USTR) (2002), *Trade Facts: United States Proposes a Tariff-Free World*, USTR, Washington, D.C., 26 November 2002.

———— (2004), Council of the Americas, Remarks of USTR Robert B. Zoellick (retrieved from http://www.ustr.gov/Document_Library/USTR_Zoellick_Speeches/2004/Council_of_the_Americas,_Remarks_of_USTR_Robert_B._Zoellick.html).

Viner, Jacob (1950), *The Customs Union Issue*, Carnegie Endowment for International Peace, New York and London: Stevens & Sons.

von Carlowitz, Philipp (2003), *Regionalismus in der Weltwirtschaft*, Schriftenreihe Volkswirtschaftliche Forschungsergebnisse, Bd. 85, Hamburg: Verlag Dr. Kovač.

Winters, L. Alan (1999), "Regionalism vs. Multilateralism" in Richard E. Baldwin, Daniel Cohen, Andre Sapir and Anthony J. Venables (eds), *Market Integration, Regionalism, and the Global Economy*, Cambridge, MA: Cambridge University Press, pp. 7-52.

Woolcock, Stephen (2003), "The Singapore Issues in Cancún: A Failed Negotiation Ploy or a Litmus Test for Global Governance?", *Intereconomics*, Vol. 38, Heft 5, pp. 249-55.

World Bank (ed.) (2000), *Trade Blocs*, Policy Research Report, World Bank, Washington, D.C.

———— (2003a), *Global Economic Prospects – Trade, Regionalism, and Development*, World Bank, Washington, D.C.

———— (2003b), *World Development Indicators (WDI) 2003*, CD-ROM, World Bank, Washington, D.C.

———— (2004), *Global Economic Prospects – Trade, Regionalism, and Development*, World Bank, Washington, D.C.

World Trade Organisation (WTO) (ed.) (2003a), *The Changing Landscape of RTAS*, paper prepared for the Seminar on Regional Trade Agreements and the WTO, 14 November 2003, WTO, Geneva.

———— (ed.) (2003b), *World Trade Report 2003*, WTO, Geneva.

———— (ed.) (2004), *Regional Trade Agreements*, WTO, Geneva (retrieved from http://www.wto.org/english/tratop_e/region_e/region_e.htm).

Zimmermann, Ralf (1999), *Regionale Integration und multilaterale Handelsordnung*, Untersuchungen zur Wirtschaftspolitik, No. 115, Institut für Wirtschaftspolitik an der Universität zu Köln, Cologne.